DESIGNING
PRODUCTIVE
LEARNING
ENVIRONMENTS

DESIGNING PRODUCTIVE LEARNING ENVIRONMENTS

FREDERICK G. KNIRK
UNIVERSITY OF SOUTHERN CALIFORNIA

Educational Technology Publications
Englewood Cliffs, New Jersey 07632

106835

Library of Congress Cataloging in Publication Data

Knirk, Frederick G
  Designing productive learning environments.

  Bibliography: p.
  Includes index.
  1. School facilities—Planning. 2. School
environment. 3. Educational technology. I. Title.
LB3261.K58   371.6'2   79-4031
ISBN 0-87778-137-0

Printed in the United States of America.

Library of Congress Catalog Card Number:
79-4031.

International Standard Book Number:
0-87778-137-0.

First Printing: July, 1979.

.

TO

Pat Knirk for her patience, encouragement, and for correcting the typewriter's spelling problem. Many thanks also to Rhoda Casey for her editing and thought-provoking questioning.

Preface

Students are ever-changing; the knowledge base continues to increase at a rapid rate; instructional techniques and materials are in flux; and social objectives around the world seem to be in turmoil. The learning environment—school buildings, classrooms, carrels, labs, playgrounds, study areas in homes—must permit and encourage an educational program in the midst of these changes. The teaching-learning facilities must also have the potential to serve the amorphous future as well.

This book is concerned with the design of *productive* spaces in schools—environments which actively encourage and facilitate learning. Educators throughout the world must take into consideration a host of human and material parameters if they want to create productive learning environments which lead to effective and efficient instruction and learning. Design and implementation must result in a series of learning areas which are conducive to learning. Frank Lloyd Wright said of inadequate architectural designs, "A doctor can bury his mistakes but an architect can only advise his client to plant vines." We already have too many irrelevant, ivy-covered buildings. We need productive, not neutral or inhibiting, learning environments. This volume is an attempt to show how to bring about such learning spaces and facilities.

F.G.K.
February, 1979

Contents

Preface vii

1. Facility Surveys and Forecasts 3

2. Learning Space Specifications 13

3. Translating Learning Specifications into Architectural
   Specifications 33

4. Site Planning and Development for New Facilities 49

5. Costs and Funding of New Facilities 55

6. The Thermal Environment 63

7. Acoustical Control 79

8. Light Control 85

9. Instructional Media Technology Requirements for Effective and Efficient Learning 97

10. Special-Purpose Facilities for More Productive Learning 115

11. Equipping the Learning Environment 125

Appendix A: Evaluation of Existing School Facilities 135

Appendix B: Checklist for Identifying Facility Requirements 139

Appendix C: Planning Checklist 143

Appendix D: Summary of Existing Facilities 147

Appendix E: Summary of Alternative Uses of Existing Facilities 149

Appendix F: Architect Selection Checklist 151

Appendix G: Carrel, Furniture, and Media Suppliers 155

Bibliography 161

Glossary 165

Index 169

DESIGNING PRODUCTIVE LEARNING
ENVIRONMENTS

Chapter One

Facility Surveys and Forecasts

The primary reason for constructing a school is to provide favorable, productive conditions for learning. A log "chair" in the middle of a forest might be the most appropriate environment for studying birds, but it isn't suitable for studying math on a cold, wet, windy afternoon.

The adequacy of any building to serve its users depends on the structure's *interior design.* A school building and its facilities should be designed from the learner or program requirements provided to the architects by educators. The educators must base their requirements on a school need survey. This can be done by analyzing existing facilities in terms of current and projected educational requirements. This analysis must include a detailed examination of many variables, including existing and projected school age population, curricula, goals of instruction, and economic limitations.

A systematic approach to performing a school need survey and forecasting the requirement for new or remodeled facilities is summarized in Figure 1.1. This procedure, like any scientifically oriented study, consists of *defining the problem, collecting data*

3

Figure 1.1

Facilities Planning

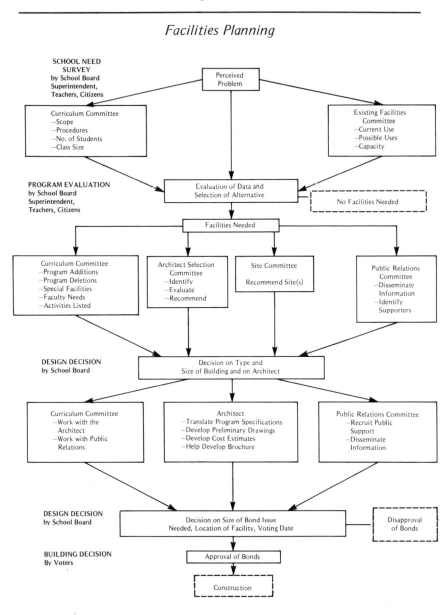

SCHOOL NEED
SURVEY
by School Board
Superintendent,
Teachers, Citizens

Perceived
Problem

Curriculum Committee
—Scope
—Procedures
—No. of Students
—Class Size

Existing Facilities
Committee
—Current Use
—Possible Uses
—Capacity

PROGRAM EVALUATION
by School Board
Superintendent,
Teachers, Citizens

Evaluation of Data and
Selection of Alternative

No Facilities Needed

Facilities Needed

Curriculum Committee
—Program Additions
—Program Deletions
—Special Facilities
—Faculty Needs
—Activities Listed

Architect Selection
Committee
—Identify
—Evaluate
—Recommend

Site Committee

Recommend Site(s)

Public Relations
Committee
—Disseminate
Information
—Identify
Supporters

DESIGN DECISION
by School Board

Decision on Type and
Size of Building and on Architect

Curriculum Committee
—Work with the
Architect
—Work with Public
Relations

Architect
—Translate Program Specifications
—Develop Preliminary Drawings
—Develop Cost Estimates
—Help Develop Brochure

Public Relations Committee
—Recruit Public
Support
—Disseminate
Information

DESIGN DECISION
by School Board

Decision on Size of Bond Issue
Needed, Location of Facility, Voting Date

Disapproval
of Bonds

BUILDING DECISION
By Voters

Approval of Bonds

Construction

on it, identifying the alternatives, and *selecting the "best" alternative.* Planning should be done by committees for curriculum and facilities. Legal, political, economic, and human considerations must be included in the survey, as well as:

(1) present and projected pupil population;

(2) educational philosophies of the teachers, administrators, and current school board members;

(3) present and projected curriculum, methods, and materials trends;

(4) evaluation of existing facilities;

(5) community needs for adult education, library, meeting, or recreation facilities;

(6) financial resources of the community; and

(7) possible expanded or new building sites.

The procedure suggested in Figure 1.1 frequently must be modified due to precedents, readily available data, and/or because public support is already behind the building program.

It is difficult to plan for the future. The use of brainstorming, "Delphi" forecasting techniques, data from the "city planning commission," "zoning boards," and state education department members should be incorporated in this prediction activity. While it is difficult to project what the future will look like, educational planners must make their best guesses, based on factual data.

The local school board, in the United States, has the responsibility for adopting policy regarding this program. The board will usually depend on the superintendent and his or her staff for recommendations. Qualified educational consultants with experience in program analysis and planning may be of assistance in this process.

Planning assistance will usually be provided by state education agencies. In some states, the "division of educational facilities planning" must be involved in planning, as it serves as a regulatory agency.

There is no better time for effecting curriculum change than when planning new or remodeled facilities. Appendix A provides a

checklist for the evaluation of existing schools. Appendix B is a
checklist of desired facilities and equipment. Appendix C is a
summary checklist for committee planning purposes. Check with
the appropriate governmental agencies for guidelines or requirements they may have. The interior instructional spaces should be
arranged to make the best possible, most productive use of every
inch.

It is important to encourage active participation by the public
during the entire planning stage. They should be included on all
committees when possible.

Recommended Procedures

As committees complete their studies, they should write reports
of findings and recommendations. Recommendations should relate
to student needs in light of the school's instructional objectives.

After data from survey committees have been collected and
reported, they should be discussed at a school board meeting, and
a decision should be made to build, to remodel existing facilities,
or to do nothing. If the decision is to build new facilities, then
four working committees need to be established: curriculum,
architect selection, site, and public relations.

The activities of these committees have been summarized in
Figure 1.1. The curriculum committee tasks are explained in more
detail in Chapter Two, Learning Space Specifications. Chapter
Four, Site Planning and Development for New Facilities, expands
on the problems to be considered by the site committee. The
public relations committee needs to begin an information dissemi-
nation program aimed at the voters.

All elements of the survey and design problem need to be seen
as they relate to each other (see Figure 1.2).

Educational consultants may be called in at this time so that the
school board may have access to the experience and knowledge of
these specialists. Qualified educational specialists may be obtained
from educational consulting firms, or for some purposes from
state education departments. Graduate colleges of education often

Figure 1.2

Survey and Design Elements

have experienced educational consultants in the field of facilities design. Do not be misled by the prestige of the institution, however, as you will usually hire an *individual* and not the *institution*. The consultant can assist on the planning of the proposed building, the formulation of the educational programs, and the selection of the architect or site. He or she can help establish:

(1) program specifications (including the number and type of spaces required);
(2) the sizes and special features of the individual spaces;
(3) the relationship of the spaces;
(4) multiple use of space for greater economy; and
(5) how to plan for instructional media.

The consultant may review preliminary sketches and progress prints of the proposed building and may be able to advise the school board of possible improvements related to pupil safety, health, instructional efficiency, flexibility, utility for adult or evening programs, integration with state programs for instructional television or other media, and the need and content of a teacher training program related to the educational philosophy to be incorporated in the facilities. He or she may continually ask questions of the school board related to the current and projected uses of the building.

If the facility need survey indicates that instructional facilities are required, either new or remodeled, the search for an architect may begin. The more information an architect is given concerning the needed space and the instructional goals and objectives, the better he or she can develop a building meeting those educational requirements.

An architect should be selected with care. He or she is the individual who will translate educational specifications into a "fixed" design. His or her professional reputation and references should be carefully examined. The selection of an architect by the board should take place after the architect selection committee has visited schools recently designed by the architect. Appendix F is a checklist to be used in comparing the qualifications of architects.

The successful development of facilities from educational specifications involves the identification and management of an extremely large amount of information. The identification of educational specifications, as discussed earlier, comes from many divergent sources: the needs, interests, desires, and expectations of the school board, school administrators, citizens, teachers, and students.

The *architect,* once selected, will examine and begin translating the educational specifications, *assist in site evaluations, prepare preliminary plans, develop cost estimates,* and *help in developing a brochure* to explain the need for the new or remodeled facilities before the community votes on the funds required for construction. The architect's responsibilities will be further discussed in Chapter Three, Translating Learning Specifications into Architectural Specifications.

The curriculum committee provides feedback and data to the architect as he or she translates the program specifications into architectural specifications and working drawings. The curriculum committee can also assist the public relations committee by providing information about the prospective programs the new facilities will support.

The school board must decide on the size of the bond issue, using data supplied by the architect. They must decide on the site and start negotiations to buy the land, if new buildings are required. Voting problems must be resolved and the vote arranged. *If the voters approve the bond issue,* the architect develops detailed plans.

Remodeling Existing Facilities

The rehabilitation, modernization, or retrofitting of existing educational facilities is a continual process. In some cases, this process may simply involve the carpeting of a classroom for a teacher who desires to make better use of the area, or it may involve the transforming of an aging elementary school with its "miniaturized facilities" into an attractive, usable intermediate school. Some projects involve extensive readjustment of the interior walls in a building, while others may involve only "preventive maintenance." Remodeling projects are often done to accommodate new functions or programs in an existing building.

An impetus for initiating these projects today often begins with the desire to improve existing schools to save energy. Other projects are begun to meet changing building codes or legal requirements. Legislation requiring the building of access ramps for physically handicapped students has resulted in some remodeling projects. If vandalism is a problem, remodeling to attract evening community activities may be considered. Finally, but perhaps of most importance to the students, new educational facilities often are required to meet the learning needs of today. As times change, so does the curriculum—and thus, so must the facilities which support this curriculum be modified.

It is especially important to involve the local community in remodeling projects, as they may have strong emotional feelings about their "old" school and its adequacy for the future.

The better the translation of program to space requirements can be accomplished, the more productive will be the educational specifications; and the better the educational specifications, the easier it is for the architect to design new spaces within an old building.

An energy crisis encourages a new appreciation of older, well-constructed buildings with their high ceilings and windows which can be opened to allow ventilation. Increasingly, well-known architects are becoming interested in remodeling and modernization projects.

Age is becoming less an indicator of obsolescence. The adaptability and safety of the building are becoming more appreciated. In many instances, a school may change hands, as from a high school to a community college, because of changing student characteristics or academic requirements. A well-designed and constructed building will be flexible and permit the rearrangement of interior spaces.

Remodeling must be a part of a total facilities need survey. This survey should be tied to a long-range analysis which includes a school need survey and a program evaluation. Both building deficiencies (structural, safety, mechanical, code) and learning limitations (spaces that are unusable in meeting the desired educational functions) should be included in the "need" survey. The decision to remodel or to build a new facility can be made after the surveys have been completed and cost estimates of the alternatives have been made.

It is often more economical to keep offices and classrooms in existing buildings and construct specialized spaces, such as gymnasiums, auditoriums, and cafeterias, in new spaces because they require specialized plumbing, electrical, ventilation, and other services. Contractors are concerned about unforeseen problems in remodeling projects which can affect their cost estimates. Keeping service changes to a minimum will reduce the contractors' uncertainty and will result in better participation and sounder cost estimates.

The "new is better" attitude is being wisely examined today. Voters seem to be more willing to support remodeling or modernization projects than new buildings. The glass and aluminum buildings of the last 25 years, which require a lot of maintenance, make the initial cost savings (when compared to brick and precast concrete structures) look less desirable now than they did when the buildings were constructed. Because of voter attitudes toward new buildings, it is often desirable to have fund raising drives for *combined* remodeling and new construction projects.

Key Points
1. The design of a school and its interior facilities and spaces can either help or hinder the teaching-learning process.
2. Surveys of "existing facilities" and of "needed facilities" should

be a regular part of the administrative facilities planning activity.

3. Remodeling of existing facilities should occur as a result of comprehensive "need" surveys.

Chapter Two

Learning Space Specifications

The *systematic* design of learning environments is essential. Systems analysis and instructional design procedures can be used to develop facilities for either specific or flexible learning activities. The detailed formulation of "educational specifications" for a new or remodeled building is accomplished after the facilities and population surveys have indicated that the new or remodeled learning environments are required.

The need for detailed attention to the design of learning spaces was brought to our attention over 50 years ago by John Dewey. "The environment can at most only supply stimuli to call out responses . . . all direction is but redirection; it shifts the activities already going on into another channel. Unless one is cognizant of the energies which are already in operation, one's attempts at direction will almost surely go amiss."[1] Educators need to be aware of the relationship between the learning environment and student achievement.

The physical size and learning shape of the classroom, learning center, instructional resources room, library, etc., have a direct effect on the activities that go on within such areas. A long, narrow classroom makes discussion difficult. A low-ceiling, hard-floored room with posts in the middle makes for a room with "difficult" acoustics.

Most facilities design questions relate to two central matters:
1. Who are the students?
2. What should students learn?

These questions, though brief, are not easy to answer. Yet, on the answers to these two questions rest the bases for the design of all learning environments. If the spaces, facilities, and instructional media do not "fit" the answers to these questions, then truly productive (efficient and effective) learning is not possible. A curriculum committee, as discussed in Chapter One, should gather data on the curriculum questions.

The curriculum committee coordinates the study of these questions and the development of a report outlining the desired program(s) to the school board, which then makes the policy decisions. The development of the specifications this committee must generate will be discussed in this chapter. Chapter Three will then indicate how the architect uses these specifications.

All teaching activities, including team-teaching, self-contained classrooms, open classrooms, etc., must be projected as accurately as possible for the near future (three to five years) and for the medium-range future (ten to 20 years). The activities and necessary materials and equipment required by such instructional approaches or philosophies of education should be clearly identified.

Educational Specifications

There are many factors inhibiting the rational, systematic development of productive educational specifications: classroom teachers use a variety of teaching techniques and learning styles or theories; curriculum specialists disagree as to how to handle the knowledge explosion; administrators are buffeted by teacher union demands, student unrest, and community desires; and architects at times attempt to design aesthetically pleasing, award-winning buildings without concern for their function. Everyone has a different idea of what schooling should be. Finally, form should follow function, but the form must conform to local and state codes, and the community must be able to afford the form.

Despite these problems, the best possible educational specifications should be developed so that the architect will provide an adequate design solution and eventually a satisfactory building.

The checklist included as Appendix B will be useful in developing the "ed specs." The space requirements (the difference between the existing facility survey data and the facilities required according to the program survey) must reflect the educational philosophy of the teachers, administrators, and school board members. It is essential to remember that the school board legally develops the educational policies. Philosophies, teachers, and school board members change, and thus, the design of a school building should be flexible enough to permit periodic changes in the learning spaces.

Three different *types of learning activities* must be planned for: passive learning, interactive learning, and active learning.

Passive learning activities involve instructional goals in which a live or mediated teacher selects, organizes, and transmits instructional stimuli to a receptive but relatively physically inactive student. The student expends little physical energy attending to television, films, programmed instruction, language laboratories, or a teacher. The student may learn alone—at his or her pace—through a specific program reflecting current interests and needs. Or, the student may be a part of a group, from two to several hundred, who listen to a lecture or watch a television presentation. A relatively comfortable and distraction-free place to attend to stimuli is all that is required for the student to meet these "passive" instructional objectives.

Due to the *presentational focus of passive learning*, conduits should be incorporated in the building to permit immediate or future installation of television, computer terminals (see Figure

2.1), dial-access, or other electronically distributed materials. Large-group areas or individualized spaces should be provided— depending upon the curriculum focus. Instructional materials and storage areas are necessary. Conveniently located instructional materials centers are desirable if much individualized work is to be done by the students.

Passive learning activities must permit the convenient use of expository materials. Projection equipment and screens must be located for easy access and student viewing. Light and sound control needed for projectors and sound amplifiers must be considered.

Learning spaces for passive activities are not content dedicated. A lecture room can be used easily for mathematics, literature, or homemaking. Charts and other graphic materials may be located in movable racks, on overhead transparencies, or reduced to slides (in this way, they do not interfere with learning activities in which they are not to be utilized).

An electronic, or language, laboratory can easily transmit symphonies, lectures, speech sounds, or political talks. Self-contained classrooms for "reaction" learning activities, following a passive situation, may need sinks if art, science, or other water-related activities are desired.

Interactive learning activities are identified by objectives involving the *interchange of concepts, facts, or data by the learners.* These activities usually occur in small groups, since all of the learners are expected to participate. The teacher's role involves stimulating the students, being a resource person, and acting as a fellow participant. Seminar or interactive areas should be provided where the students and teachers can debate a point without disturbing others. These activities are usually related to one of the other two types of learning activities, which provide the cognitive data for the interaction.

People interact with each other in nonverbal ways. The spatial interaction which we design into our learning spaces may violate an individual's "personal territory," and this close proximity may

Figure 2.1

Students at Computer Terminal

Photo Credit: International Business Machines Corporation (IBM).

make him or her uncomfortable and inhibit his or her ability to concentrate on interactive learning activities. Hall and others have identified how individuals require different kinds and amounts of personal space.[2,3,4] Learning spaces with too little square footage for the learners will result in conflict and tension. See Chapter Eleven for recommendations on the selection and placement of furnishings to promote interactive instructional goals.

Active learning activities are related to objectives requiring the student to "learn by doing." These are usually space-consuming activities. Cognitive, affective, and psychomotor objectives may require individual and group spaces. Programmed materials requiring continuous individual activity may be used to aid the students. The use of programmed materials to attain objectives requiring students to be active is illustrated by an instructional area designed to aid in teaching biology. The students are required to listen to programmed audiotapes which leave their hands free to use the microscope, to dissect, to draw, to take notes, to turn pages in their manual, etc. The program can direct the student to leave his or her carrel with its microscope and tape deck to go to the greenhouse, chemical area, demonstration setting, small-group discussion area (for interactive activities) and to the lecture hall (for the more physically passive learning activities). Centrally located instructional materials centers permit easy access to desired materials.

The different types of learning activities have somewhat different space requirements. The relationship or proximity of these spaces needs to be considered. Where should the activity spaces (e.g., those needed physical education areas, music practice rooms, or shops) be located in relation to the instructional spaces required for other learning activities?

Some students may be hyperactive and/or for other reasons over-react to high-stimulus environments. These individuals require different facilities than other students.[5]

Individualized Learning Facilities

Individualized instruction space requirements are quite different from those necessary for self-contained classrooms or team-teaching. The traditional facilities—classroom, library, study hall—do not provide the spaces which encourage independent study. Traditional designs do not have places for study, places to work unbothered by others, places to meet in small groups, or places to consult individually with teachers. Independent study requires the following learning environments:

    (1) instructional materials center;
    (2) library;
    (3) conference areas;
    (4) relaxation space; and
    (5) formal study areas.

The materials center is designed for study, active work, and conversing. The library is intended for students needing specialized resources. Conference areas permit and encourage teacher-student discussions, student interaction, teacher-directed instruction, or teacher-directed study. The formal study will be done by many students in carrels (often, a carrel is permanently assigned to each student—his or her own office). Projectors and tape recorders with earphones are frequently used in the carrels. The set of relationships suggested in Figure 2.2 would provide an environment supporting many individualized instruction programs. The design of spaces to permit such areas must be flexible and may take many shapes. Separate the quiet areas from the noisy ones.

Individualized instruction is facilitated by an area where individual students can obtain and study resource materials. There should be places where groups of students can get together and discuss what they are doing without disturbing other learners. It may be desirable to provide for large-group instruction, even in a program which is primarily individualized. If it becomes desirable to teach unprogrammed concepts or to permit a guest lecturer to talk to the students, group instructional areas will be needed.

In discussing *nongraded* instructional procedures, John Goodlad and Robert Anderson endorse "... a combination of grouping procedures accompanied by a variety of evaluative devices ... planned flexibility in grouping is a key to maximum pupil growth."[6] The school environment must allow, and should encourage, such groupings *by its design.*

Team-Teaching Facilities

Team-teaching often requires instructional areas of conventional size having the flexibility to be immediately expanded or contracted to permit a larger or smaller number of students to work with a particular teacher at a given time. Students in an independent study science program might be able to use their carrel spaces for experiments, or they may need to have laboratory facilities offering access to specialized materials and equipment. Students working on *group* projects will need other spaces.

Old buildings, or new buildings with rigid spaces, as in Figure 2.3a, inhibit team-teaching activities. Figures 2.3b and 2.3c suggest ways of providing flexible open spaces unlimited by interior walls. The dashed lines reflect group instruction areas without fixed interior walls. The spaces in an "open" building would permit:

Figure 2.2

An Individualized Instruction Area

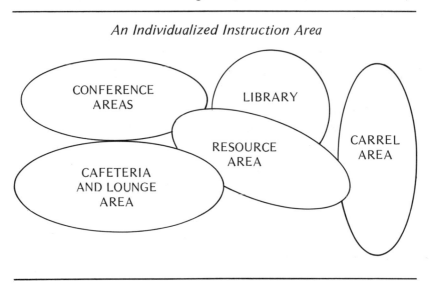

Figure 2.3

Alternative Classroom Space Designs

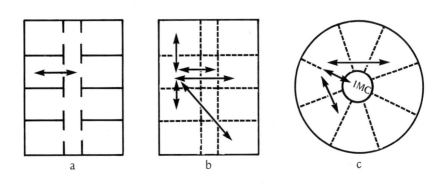

(1) the accommodation of groups of various sizes—from one or two students to many;

(2) rapid shifting of group size; and

(3) teachers to have a place where they can work privately or consult with individuals or prepare instructional lessons and materials.

In addition to more flexible learning and teacher work spaces, team-teaching programs often require a centrally located library or instructional materials center (IMC). These centrally situated areas permit students to use such resources easily and constantly with little travel time or loss of teacher control. Team-teaching facilities often have the IMC centrally located so that it is convenient to all students and teachers.

Schools which are primarily team-teaching oriented often have conventional spaces for a Kindergarten (if an elementary school), and physical education, art, music, and auditorium or multi-purpose rooms (which may frequently be used as large-group instructional areas). The design of a team-teaching facility, like any other, requires a study of probable curriculum practices and materials to be used in the facility. In addition, the building should be designed with the capability to be changed to permit other, future curriculum, student grouping, or presentational practices.

Self-Contained Classrooms

If self-contained classrooms are desired, a set of questions needs to be asked:

1. What number of which types of classroom facilities are needed?

2. What types of learning activities are expected to take place in these classrooms? Passive? Active? Interactive? Individualized to any degree?

3. Are. sinks, drinking fountains, and/or toilets to be in or adjoining each classroom?

4. Is natural lighting to be supplemented by artificial

lighting?

5. Should movable partitions separate adjoining instructional spaces?

The architecture itself can sort children. It can help the administration to establish groups of uniform size with relatively homogeneous abilities. Self-contained classrooms may or may not have four walls surrounding the teacher and his or her students.

Social Environments

Learning in schools occurs in social settings. This social environment thus becomes an important aspect of productive learning facilities design. An effective social environment, like any learning environment, should promote immediate and positive feedback to the individual about his or her ideas and their acceptance. The individual's self-concept should be enhanced in school. Increased openness or sensitivity will encourage a student to value peers and teachers. This valuing will tend to permit him or her to perceive more stimuli in the environment and thus to "grow" more quickly intellectually and emotionally.

A classroom itself is a medium of communications. The students react to it. A "hard classroom" with cement or tile floors, with hard plaster walls and ceilings, and with hard-surfaced furniture makes a classroom a very *formal* environment. The classroom communicates *affective* data. The student often perceives that he or she can make little impression on it. He or she must be a relatively passive receptor. The student is often encouraged to behave passively because of one-at-a-time class recitation and passive learning activities. The student's seated position, as opposed to a standing and more dominant position used by the teacher, further reduces interaction and may affect the student's impression of his or her own worth. The environment, thus, becomes intimidating and destructive rather than encouraging and productive. Attitudes toward schooling often are different where the furniture is soft and the student is encouraged to actively promote his or her own schooling. Austere instructional spaces should give way to an environment reflecting other areas of the child's life-space.

The learning environment must facilitate the perception of desired (problem-related, tension-reducing, pleasure-producing) stimuli and inhibit undesired (confusing, unordered) stimuli.

A facility which permits easy movement and a diffuse structure may promote the development of a positive self-concept. An individual should have some freedom of mobility to avoid threatening groups or situations. A student needs to be able to isolate himself or herself to resolve personal problems.

Some large schools have created a number of "houses" in order to obtain the economic advantages of large physical size without losing the intimacy offered by small schools. These "schools within a school" allow for continued student social and academic contact with a limited number of students and teachers. Figure 2.4 illustrates one way to relate or arrange the "houses" to obtain the economic advantages possible in a large building.

Translating Specifications to Designs

The trend in the United States toward the use of team-teaching, individualized instruction, and mediated instructional technology requires that educators write specifications which call for more open architectural specifications and designs. Architectural specifications or solutions from educational specifications could develop, for example, as follows:

1. The building should hold 160 K-3 students in groups of 20. There should be two teaching stations for each of the four grades.
2. The instructional curriculum will be presented or taught using team-teaching and differentiated staffing techniques requiring easy student movement between teaching stations.
3. Heavy use of books and other instructional materials requires easy access to an instructional materials center.
4. Frequent student location changes and revisions in group

Figure 2.4

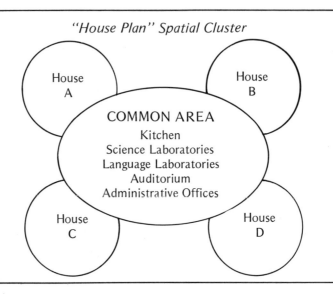

"House Plan" Spatial Cluster

House
A

House
B

COMMON AREA
Kitchen
Science Laboratories
Language Laboratories
Auditorium
Administrative Offices

House
C

House
D

size require furniture and furnishings which will not affect the expansion or contraction of the teaching-learning areas.
5. The building should be flexible enough to permit easy future curriculum related space changes.
6. The building will be used for summer school and evening adult education activities.
7. The building should be as inexpensive as possible and yet contribute to the appearance of the neighborhood.

Open teaching-learning space specifications require some visual and acoustical control if directed learning is to occur. Noise reduction, when chairs are moved, might be met, in part, by the use of carpeting. The visual control requirement might be met by placing storage racks, coat hooks, or book cases (placed on casters) in appropriate locations.

The interior design of the building may be made more flexible if there are no perimeter windows to restrict the movement of partitions. The design of windowless classrooms may require air conditioning. The utilities (e.g., electrical outlets) should also be installed to produce little restriction of the internal space arrangements.

An instructional materials room placed near the center of the building would permit implementation of the educational specification requiring individual students to have easy access to book and non-text materials. The desirability of such centrally located facilities suggests the design of round buildings, as in Figure 2.5, which minimizes the distance to the instructional materials area.

Classrooms which are carpeted and have air conditioning are easily modified to permit more conventional instruction or other instructional methods as they are desired in the future.

The key architectural specifications derived from these sample educational specifications include:

(1) a centrally located "instructional materials center" in a round building;
(2) a windowless, partitionless design;
(3) an air conditioned building;
(4) movable internal partitions between teaching stations;
(5) movable furniture and furnishings;
(6) carpeting in the teaching areas and corridors; and
(7) easily accessible electricity (as in floor channels) and other services which will permit easy redesign of the internal space.

Remember, these architectural designs were used *only* as a simplified illustration-example, showing the use of educational specifications by an architect. These are *not* the only, nor necessarily the best, translations of the educational specifications.

The educational specifications, in summary, should result from an examination of these three general questions:

(1) how and when will the individual student work or learn;
(2) what resources will be and/or should be available to the teacher and student; and
(3) what should be the teacher and student roles in the teaching-learning system (who is responsible for selection

106835

Figure 2.5

Open Plan Elementary School

of content; who is responsible for learning failures or successes; who is responsible for developing motivation or interest; how is the "scientific approach" to problem-solving developed; by whom, when, and how often should the student work by himself or herself, with a partner, or others, with a small group having a student leader, with a dozen students and a teacher, and/or in a large group)?

The educational specifications must include physical descriptions related to acoustics, lighting, sanitation, safety, ventilation, interior decoration, and internal flexibility; provisions for future expansion; chalkboards or other facilities; special instructional equipment; sizes of classrooms and other spaces; and provisions for presentation (expository teaching), independent work, investigation, drill, discussion, simulation, and role playing when desired.

Administrative and learning spaces must be seen as functional units or clusters. The administration cluster, for example, involves the location and relationships of the general office, the principal's office, the assistant principal's office, the guidance office, the health office, and the main lobby. Figure 2.6 graphically illustrates this cluster.

The service cluster must relate these activities: general storage; receiving; incinerator; custodians' work shop; storage of outdoor equipment; etc. Each of the content areas will also have clusters. For example, the homemaking cluster should involve the general homemaking, nursery, living center, and cooking areas.

Safety, Codes, and Regulations

Educational specifications requiring healthful and safe facilities are essential. The welfare of the students, as translated to school design and construction, is governed by state and local codes. No type of construction or construction materials should be used which might endanger the safety, health, or comfort of the students. Of the many apparent alternatives open for the use of the educational dollar, none is acceptable unless the health and safety of the student is assured.

The educational specifications may include warnings about the door "swing" area, stairs, handrails, floor surfaces, glass panels, etc. The specifications may require that all areas be accessible to the physically handicapped. Ramps into the building may be required in addition to steps. If so, the angle of the ramp and the curbing should allow easy and safe use.

Fire-resistant materials should always be used. Corridors should be relatively wide and free of obstructions. All points along a corridor should be within about 150 feet (50 meters) of an exit. On the floors above the ground floor, less distance should exist between any point on the corridor and the exit stairway. Exact corridor width minimums will be specified by local and state codes. These minimums will vary depending on the number of students in the building and the age of the students. Loft plan, or other "open plan" schools, which do not have corridors in the traditional sense, should be designed so that no student will have to travel over 100 feet (33 meters) to an exit.

Figure 2.6

Administration Functions Cluster

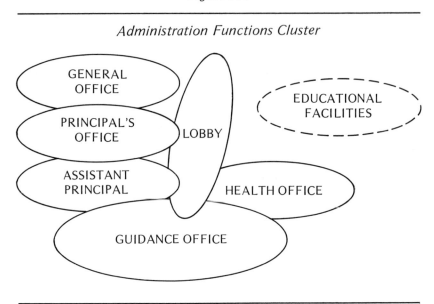

There should be at least two remotely separated exits from all learning spaces. A student should have a choice of two means of exiting a burning building. Every classroom should have two exits. The primary exit may be through the classroom door; the secondary exit might be through a window. Exit doors directly to the outside are desirable when security, design, and economic factors permit. Windowless classrooms reduce the number of potential exits, so the architect must plan for suitable alternative emergency exits.

Potential fire or explosion hazards originating in the "furnace room" can be reduced through the use of many electrical and mechanical safety systems. These are generally well specified by local building codes.

Sanitation, like fire safety, is strictly governed by local and state regulations. Water supply and discharge are of special concern to the architect in evaluating the potential of a school site.

The use and maintenance of grease and oil traps in the kitchens, art rooms, and garages may be necessary. The architect will also be concerned with the design, location, and number of toilet facilities. He or she must also be concerned about the ventilation of the toilet areas and special areas, such as chemistry laboratories. Drinking fountains should not be located in the toilet areas, and should be constructed of impervious materials.

The *furnishings* should be selected for their safety. Shelving with sharp corners, armchairs with movable pieces which could pinch, top heavy and unstable tables, glass covers on specimen jars, pencil sharpeners located behind doors, and other similar potential hazards should be eliminated before they cause an injury. All edges should be rounded, smooth, or padded.

Playground equipment should be located with ample space between pieces. Swings and merry-go-rounds are dangerous unless well-supervised. Moving parts, as at the fulcrum of a teeter-totter, should have safety guards. Hard surfaces should have soft sanitary padding whenever possible. For beginning swimmers, a swimming pool should have an "end" of about 30 to 40 inches deep. Recreational swimming areas for advanced swimmers should range from 42 to 50 inches (107 to 127 cm) in depth. Diving or competitive pools must meet additional depth standards. The floor around the pools should be sloped to drain away from the pool and should be composed of, or covered with, a non-slip material. The locker room and shower area should also be covered with non-slip materials. Automatic water-temperature controls will eliminate the possibility of scalding.

The *science laboratory* areas need special attention with regard to safety. If toxic or volatile materials are to be used, adequate fume hoods must be built into the laboratories. Chemicals which react violently should be isolated whenever possible. Electrical outlets for student use in the laboratories need to be adequately fused and their controls easily accessible to the teachers. Fire extinguishers should be available in all laboratories.

Industrial arts or shop areas also require special design attention from a safety standpoint. Sufficient lighting for the tasks to be performed is essential. Each activity should have sufficient space, and there should be unobstructed visibility in the area. Secure storage for chemicals must be provided. The flooring should be smooth with no power or control cables located on it. Dangerous moving or projecting parts should be color-coded on the equipment or on the floor, or both.

The *school site* may also present hazards to student health and safety. Play areas should be properly drained to insure fast, even drying. Eroded areas or cliffs should be marked and/or fenced off. Power lines should be underground near the school, if possible, to eliminate hazards to after-school students using the grounds for kite or model plane flying. The staff and student parking, the bus loading area, and the traffic patterns must be such that students will not have to, or be tempted to, walk into areas where the cars or buses will be moving. Off-street parking is highly desirable. The architect and the educators should work together toward reducing these and similar problems. Ventilation, lighting, and acoustical hazards are also of concern but are discussed in detail elsewhere in this book.

School boards get their authority from the statutes of the state and can exercise no powers except as granted. School districts may not expend funds for school construction except as expressly authorized by statute, so the boards need to be aware of the legal implications of their decisions.

Building codes and regulations are designed to protect the public against inadequate designs and construction techniques or materials. Building codes and other regulations have a significant impact on the freedom of building design and on the cost of a project. Specifically, building codes regulate construction materials, foundation and structural loads, building height, fireproofing, plumbing installation and fixtures, electrical installation, heating equipment, and elevator designs and devices. Some agencies or codes to consider when building in the United States are these: Occupational Safety and Health Act (OSHA), Environmental Protection Agency, Uniform Building Code, National Electric

Code, National Plumbing Code, and the Uniform Mechanical Code. State or local codes usually cover: Requirements for the Physically Handicapped, Fire Safety, Earthquake/Hurricane/Tornado Safety, Health and Sanitation, Water Pollution, and Air Pollution.

Conclusion

The purpose of a school building is to actively encourage the desired educational program. A curriculum study should result in learning specifications, which are the bases for architectural specifications. A study of facility needs must involve an impartial overview of the facilities and requirements of the entire school district. The educational facilities must provide for population shifts and cultural requirements. Just how this is accomplished is not as simple as "1, 2, 3," but it must be attempted. The recommendations for building new facilities or for remodeling old facilities must be financially realistic and reflect the data from which these conclusions were derived.

Learner space requirements should allow and encourage:

(1) flexibility and multiple use of spaces;
(2) various sized groups ranging from two to several hundred;
(3) individual student study areas with visual and acoustical privacy;
(4) access to a wide range of instructional materials; and
(5) space which is affectively pleasing and psychologically supportive of learning.

In order to implement such school surveys and space specifications, it is desirable to involve the community in the planning process. The involvement will provide data from the community relative to their perceived curriculum needs. This involvement usually results in more support for the bond issue when the time comes to vote on the funds.

In order to get firsthand knowledge about the way the new school designs meet the varying educational specifications, visit some exemplary schools in your area. Use Appendix A as a guide on these visits. Talk with the principal, teachers, students, and the custodians.

Key Points

1. The curriculum determines the activities and functions to be housed in the school. Form should follow function.
2. There are three generalized types of learning activities: passive, active, and interactive. Each type of activity requires specialized spaces.
3. Individualized learning and team-teaching activities require large open and flexible areas to contain these programs.
4. Educational specifications defined by educators are used by architects to develop architectural specifications.
5. Related functions should be clustered together, whenever possible.
6. Safety considerations, usually found in codes and regulations, are over-riding considerations.

Notes

1. Dewey, John. *Democracy and Education.* New York: Macmillan, 1916, pp. 25-26.

2. Hall, Edward. *The Silent Language.* New York: Doubleday and Company, 1959.

3. Sommer, Robert. *Personal Space: The Behavioral Basis of Design.* Englewood Cliffs, N.J.: Prentice-Hall, Inc., 1969.

4. Galloway, Charles. *Silent Language in the Classroom.* Bloomington, Indiana: Phi Delta Kappa Educational Foundation, 1976.

5. Cruickshank, W., and Johnson, G. *Education of Exceptional Children and Youth.* New York: Prentice-Hall, Inc., 1967, p. 273.

6. Goodlad, John, and Anderson, Robert. *The Nongraded Elementary School.* New York: Harcourt, Brace, and World, Inc., 1949, p. 99.

Chapter Three

Translating Learning Specifications into Architectural Specifications

Educators should analyze the teaching-learning and administrative functions to be contained in a new or a redesigned school building. Following the translation of these activities into educational specifications, they must be rewritten by the architect as architectural specifications. Educators need to identify and specify the educational activities in a manner understandable to the architect. Educators and school board members have the responsibility for locating and hiring a competent architect that can, and will, translate those learning specifications accurately.

The translation of the learning specifications into architectural specifications occurs in sequential, but overlapping, order:

(1) select the architect;

(2) give him or her the previously developed educational specifications and interact about them;

(3) select the site;

(4) prepare the preliminary plans;

(5) present the final plans, specifications, and cost estimates to the board of education;

(6) submit the final plans, specifications, and cost estimates to the voters;

(7) have the final plans reviewed and approved by the appropriate governmental agencies;

(8) accept competitive bids and awards for general contracts and sub-contracts; and, finally,

(9) begin construction activities.

The architect and his or her staff play the key role in the implementation of the educators' requirements.

The *architect's professional services* will usually include:

(1) translating the program or learning specifications into architectural specifications;

(2) preparing preliminary studies;

(3) designing working drawings and specifications;

(4) developing detailed drawings for architectural, structural, and mechanical work;

(5) assisting in the drafting of proposals and contracts;

(6) issuing certificates of payment;

(7) keeping the accounts; and

(8) supervising the construction.

The architect endeavors, but does not guarantee, to guard the board against defects in the contractor's work.

PERT (Program Evaluation and Review Technique) or other management tools are desirable to project the time line which must be met for the orderly completion of the building.

The following are desired by the architect of the educator:

(1) a definition of the educational program in language which can be understood by all parties. Avoid jargon having meaning only to educators;

(2) a statement concerning the learning requirements, including the areas and times of use. Include any atypical problems of maintenance, light, temperature, air movement, number of students, etc.; and

(3) identification of the amount of needed space and the relationship of one space to another.

Floor Plan Designs

The following educational specifications would direct an architect to consider and adopt a specific floor plan:

(1) cooling by outside air currents or by air conditioning;

(2) self-contained and/or acoustically isolated or flexible interior spaces;

(3) clusters by activity (as noise, odor—chemistry or home-making, content, etc.);

(4) multiple uses as apartments or business areas;

(5) house plan programming, calling for groups of students to work as an entity in a much larger building;

(6) multiple-story buildings; and/or

(7) specified cost levels.

An architect has several generally accepted alternative floor plans. Alternatives are illustrated in Figure 3.1.

The decision to choose a *corridor plan* design would result from educational specifications requiring windows for ventilation (as opposed to air conditioning), so as to obtain the maximum use of air currents. It would also involve self-contained or isolated teacher stations for specified numbers of students. The use of movable partitions could permit easily changing the number of students in the various areas. The isolation is fairly good without any special acoustical treatment. A disadvantage of a corridor plan building is that it is difficult to use the corridors for non-educational purposes, thus not employing space to the best advantage. This floor plan may be used in multiple-story buildings by stacking the floors one above the other—connected by stairways, of course.

A decision to build a *finger plan* school would result from specifications similar to those for a corridor plan school. The finger plan school may be viewed as a number of corridors joined together and, as such, the difference is often one of deciding to build horizontally instead of vertically. Finger plan schools are seldom over two or three stories high and are often used in one-story designs. The ventilation due to natural wind currents is more restricted than in the corridor plan because of interference from other "fingers."

Figure 3.1

Sample Floor Plans

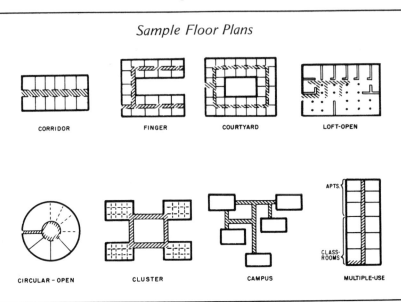

The *courtyard plan* school is another variation of the corridor plan school, and the same general specifications discussed for it apply to this design. If multiple stories are planned, special attention should be given to artificial ventilation for the rooms on the courtyard. Note that students will constantly view other students across the courtyard, and this may be a source of distraction. If plants and grass are desired in the courtyard, limit the building to a single story unless the courtyard area is quite large.

Neither the finger plan nor the courtyard plan is desirable if the building is to be air conditioned. The need to insulate the surface area of the building and the inevitable transfer of heat with a large surface make these designs undesirable.

The extensive surface area of exterior walls also increases the cost of the building. Exterior wall construction is most expensive, and the reduction of these walls will reduce the costs per square foot of the building. Thus, specifications requiring minimal expenditures will affect the decision to use "finger" plans or other plans with extensive exterior wall requirements. In urban areas, the cost of land will encourage multiple-story buildings.

The *loft plan* school offers a large amount of open space, which can be arranged or rearranged with relative ease. Specifications calling for team-teaching, with frequent student movement and group size changes, may be met by this design. Properly insulated, this building is ideal for air conditioning, as it is a compact plan. Noise (like band practice) or odors (chemistry) are more difficult to control in this plan than in the other plans thus far discussed.

A *circular plan* is usually another open design which is internally flexible. The center area may be an instructional materials center, a large-group instruction area, or an administrative center. Kindergarten and special areas, such as music rooms, may have plaster walls and special sound isolation treatments. If the center area is open, it is usually carpeted for acoustical purposes. This building, with its small perimeter area, is easy to air condition and relatively inexpensive. Usually, a circular plan building is a single story building.

The *cluster school* is ideally suited to acoustical or odor problems. These activities may be physically isolated from the rest of the school. The cluster design consumes a great amount of area, and thus, it may not be feasible in urban settings. The clusters themselves may be of varying size and may have one of the five basic floor plans previously discussed. If the clusters are content or grade related, the learning materials and supplies necessary to those grades can be met by putting the appropriate materials in the appropriate cluster. If the student population varies sufficiently to make expansion necessary beyond the intended cluster, the advantages of this plan become problems instead.

A *campus plan school* is a macro-design like the cluster plan. This plan may incorporate the corridor, finger, loft, or circular designs. The campus plan is essentially a series of schools on a single plot of ground. This plan may permit relatively easy adoption of specifications requiring the racial integration of students, since the students from a large area are brought together in one location. It may also reduce administrative, heating, and maintenance costs as fewer administrators, heating units, and maintenance personnel may be required. Busing costs will rise as the distances increase and the possibility of having the students walk home for lunch is decreased; thus, there will have to be relatively large lunch, supervision, and recreation programs.

Multiple-use facilities may result from (1) specifications requiring relatively rapid expansion or contraction of educational spaces; (2) low expenditure by the community for such space; or (3) proximity to apartments or business spaces. As the school space requirements expand, the floors "above" the "school" must be vacated by the residents or business occupants. If the school space requirements are reduced, the school may lease this area and thus increase the revenue base from which to pay off the school bonds and other costs. Multiple-use facilities are schools in buildings which also contain living and/or business offices. Such facilities have been built, for example, in New York City and Chicago. These buildings are usually high-rise structures where specific floors are used for schools, and the other floors are leased to renters. The proximity to apartments may reduce student travel expenses and problems, and/or the proximity to business offices may allow business oriented students to gain practical experiences desirable to both the leasing businesses and the school. More details on this joint occupancy arrangement are given in Chapter Five, where the economics of this approach to funding educational facilities are examined.

Interior Design Specifications

Educational specifications which are vague or involve frequent changes in the size, shape, or characteristics of instructional spaces, as in team-teaching situations, dictate a building designed for internal flexibility. This flexibility may come about with the use of few or no load-bearing walls.

Some architects obtain this flexibility through the use of

movable partitions (operable walls; folding partitions; portable walls; demountable walls; or furniture on casters). Operable walls, which are usually motor-driven, and folding partitions are similar in that they fold or compress or slide out of the way—easily. Portable walls can be moved by the school maintenance personnel—occasionally. The demountable wall usually requires special tools and fixtures and is moved by the manufacturer—very seldom. Many schools have coat racks, chalkboards, bulletin boards, and storage cabinets built into partitions on casters which can be easily pushed by teachers or students.

The sound qualities of these partitions vary considerably. Some partitions have better sound control properties than conventional walls, and others do not. In the mid-1950's, the folding walls were being built mainly for home owners desiring to visually isolate one area from another at relatively little expense. These partitions had little sound control. In the early 1960's, schools desired, and began obtaining, movable walls that did control noise.

Flexibility is possible with movable partitions if the electrical power conduits (for television or other electronic media, air ducts, and plumbing) are designed into the ceiling or floor. If they are placed in internal walls, it is difficult to modify the spaces, if desired. The technical problems of locating plumbing and electrical connections in these flexible schools are relatively simple.

Educational specifications involving air and heat control, acoustics, and lighting will be discussed in detail in Chapters Six, Seven, and Eight.

Prefabricated Units

The use of prefabricated buildings (*pre-engineered, relocatable classrooms, disposable schools*) should be considered during the translation of the educational specifications into architectural specifications. Educational specifications which call for rapid construction and/or inexpensive buildings may be met by using these units. Prefabricated units are usually pre-engineered and acquire various names because of their relatively low initial costs, rapidity of construction, and initial (and sometimes later) portability. One should not be misled simply by a promise of low initial cost. The cheapest possible first cost is not always a true indication of economy. Initial savings may soon be more than lost through abnormal costs for maintenance, replacement, or insurance. Any physical limitation that handicaps the educational program or reduces safety, sanitation, or efficiency should be classified as false economy. True economy is a complex relationship between original cost, educational utility and efficiency, and maintenance and operating expenditures. Some of the prefabricated facilities will represent the best use of your building dollars.

Many of the recent pre-engineered buildings have price tags which are comparable with buildings designed and constructed locally. What you gain by using these facilities is a lag of less than one year from the time the funds are available for purchase until the building is occupied. This time lag is often a reduction of a year or more from the conventional construction timetable. The possibilities of all-steel construction, bright and washable colors, carpeting, and relocatability as necessary are additional justifications for prefabricated buildings. These buildings are usually one-story structures but may be two- or three-story complexes.

Systems Projects

The conventional way to design and construct a school building is to design each portion—almost every brick—of the building. In the mid-1960's, several projects were begun in the United States and Canada which involved the use of prefabricated modular components to reduce construction time and decrease building costs. These are not prefabricated buildings but prefabricated and compatible *components.* These components can be ordered in "building blocks," so many different external and internal designs are possible. An architect designs the general layout and the unique units. The major components or subsystems usually are the heating-ventilating-cooling, electrical, lighting, flooring, partitioning, plumbing, and structural components.

These modules are designed to respond to almost any set of educational specifications, since all buildings require a way to control the elements (rain, snow, heat) and must be internally flexible enough to meet future educational requirements in addition to those identified for the near future. A developing country could reduce both cost and time requirements for new facilities if it used "systems" concepts in building.

The School Construction Systems Development project (SCSD), funded by the Educational Facilities Laboratories, is one example of a *systems project.*[1] This project involved the construction of 13 California schools from modular components. The use of SCSD, or other systems buildings, will reduce the architectural design requirements and decrease the time required to "construct" a building.

The Schoolhouse Systems Project (SSP) is a second-generation systems project. The cost of SSP systems buildings is about 20 percent lower than are conventional facilities, according to Florida statistics. As more users adopt these commercially available modules, it should be possible to further reduce construction costs. The Detroit Public Schools are using this system.[2]

Windowless Classrooms

Windowless classrooms may be designed to educational or economic specifications. The annual cost of replacing broken windows in schools in the United States is extremely high, with estimates generally running about 50 million dollars annually. Vandalism resulting from gaining access to the building through windows runs in the millions of dollars in most large cities.

The use of windowless classrooms reduces distractions from outside the classroom, cuts vandalism costs, and lowers initial construction expenses, as it costs more to build windows into a wall than to have windowless external walls. Windows are poor insulators, so the cost of heat or cooling increases in direct proportion to the amount of glass in a building. The painful glare of sunlight streaming into a classroom can also be eliminated by windowless school designs.

What do students and teachers think of windowless rooms? The children, in one case study, liked their windowless classrooms, mainly due to the additional bright colors on the walls and floors.[3] Without exception, the teachers stated that the absence of windows offered an advantage. They said: "There were not distractions from airplanes, nor from children playing outdoors, nor from other outside distractions; there was no direct sunlight and thus no glare; the teacher could arrange the room more ways; the room was more evenly heated and the temperature was the same over the entire room; ventilation is often better; younger children with short attention spans are less easily distracted by non-instructional 'stimuli.' "[4] The teachers' affective reactions often involved initial feelings of being closed-in. At the end of the first class year, even those teachers who had initially disliked the windowless classrooms joined the teachers who liked the window-less classrooms from the beginning.

Generally, the children's behavior was reported to be supportive of the windowless environments. One teacher said, "On pleasant days I doubt that there is much change, but there isn't the distraction with rain, snow, etc., that is common when the children can see. I don't believe overcast, dreary days cause the restlessness that sometimes occurs (with windows)."[5] Appraisal of pupil ability and achievement based on standardized tests (Iowa Test of Basic Skills and the Gates Reading Test) indicated that some children did better in a windowless environment while others did worse. It was concluded that "the close parallel in pupil learning achievement between the two schools (Experimental and Control) hardly permits any other conclusion than that classroom windows have very little or any effect on a child's ability to learn."[6]

When windowless instructional areas are constructed, it is important that adequate ventilation be provided to eliminate heat, humidity, and odors. *Air conditioning* can easily do this task. If air conditioning is not used in windowless buildings, they must have at least an air blower system. Air conditioning may often resolve educational specifications calling for year-round use of a school building. It will also result in a low pollen level and controlled humidity and thermal conditions.

Per Student Space Requirements

The total space requirement per student *depends on the activities the student is expected to perform.* In a self-contained, passive classroom which is heavily prescheduled, relatively little space is required. Specialized classrooms, such as music, art, or library areas, often require more total space per student. Smaller class enrollments also tend to increase the per student space requirement. Physical activities which occur in such places as physical education, homemaking, art, etc., require relatively more space than do passive activities.

Kindergartens are active spaces and often are designed for 1,200 square feet. The other self-contained elementary classrooms are less active and require only 900 square feet. An IMC may require 5,000 square feet for an elementary school. Data from the state education department is available to estimate the approximate size of a school building once you have estimated the number of pupils who will attend the school. In addition to classroom spaces, the service spaces, corridors, and administrative areas take their space toll.

Construction Supervision

After the architect's plans have been approved by the school board and the funds voted, the architect has the task of interpreting the architectural plans and specifications to those who do the actual building. The architect will issue, during the building process, supplementary detailed drawings and instructions about the procedures to be followed in the execution of the work. He or she must inspect all shop drawings prepared by suppliers and sub-contractors for components and assemblies to be incorporated into the building.

The board must provide for the processing of the architect's *certificate of payment.* Most contractors are appreciative of prompt payment of claims, since their obligations to sub-contractors have to be met on time.

The architect often has the responsibility of approving the contractor's application for progress payments, which represent the percentage of the work completed and the sum of money due at that point. It is a usual practice to withhold from ten to 15 percent of the payment as a guarantee of the completion of the work by the contractor.

The school board must have confidence in the architect, especially during the construction phase. This is important when change orders start to develop during the initial stages of construction. The architect should be given the authority by the school board to make immediate decisions on minor items. On larger change orders, the architect must have authority to obtain cost estimates and secure school board approval. The board should insist that all changes be in written form and that they are acted on promptly. Practically all construction jobs of any size will involve change orders, so it becomes important that school boards appropriate enough funds at the outset to take care of these contingencies.

The handling of change orders is undoubtedly one of the architect's toughest problems and one of his or her major responsibilities. This is true especially in school building construction because public funds are involved and usually the amount of money provided for change is limited. Change orders may occur because of unexpected rock, subsoil, and water problems. Changes in footings and foundations may be required because of soil and water conditions. Changes initiated by the school board or the school administration can be made, but careful planning will avoid most of these. Sometimes, there are errors in the architect's drawings. School boards should realize that human error is inevitable and should not be critical of minor errors by the architect. The average sum needed for changes ranges from two percent to five percent of the total price of the contract.

The legal contract for the *architectural services* rendered should be as specific and unambiguous as possible. This will prevent confusion and possible later litigation. Architects often provide advice as to the terms of the contract and possibly suggest a contract form. The school board, chief school administrator, and the school lawyer should examine the contract in detail. Specifically, examine the: basis of architect's fees and fees to engineers and other specialists; basis of billing for extras (travel, extra blueprints, changes after approval of plan); inspection of construction by architect; ownership of design (drawings and specifications remain professional property of architect); method of arbitrating disputes between architect and school board; and method of terminating contract, as necessary, on a basis of payment for services rendered to date.

The architect provides rough sketches, diagrams, and drawings which represent the various stages of the architect's analysis of the functions to be provided by the building. The state education department, division of educational facilities planning (or a similar name), can be of great assistance throughout this process. The architect and members of the school board should visit the division during the preparation of the preliminary plans. Generally, they must get the division's approval on the final plans.

The architect should provide complete *working drawings* covering the site plans and floor plans. These drawings should also provide details of the structural, lighting, heating, and ventilating systems. Clear-cut specifications of the details, equipment, and method of construction which can serve as the basis for competitive bids should be submitted. Final cost estimates from contractors based on these detailed specifications should also be obtained. The school board must examine and approve these *final plans.* At least 50 percent of the total architectural fee, computed as a percentage of the estimated building cost, will be due at this time. The architect must conform to *code and safety standards* of the local community and of the state. He or she will make applications for all necessary building permits. The state education department will normally review and approve all plans for educational facilities.

The architect normally supervises the *bidding* and will provide advice to the client on the evaluation of the bids and the final award of the building contract. The school board must then contract with the general contractors and sub-contractors.

In general, the architect has responsibility to provide general administration of all of the business aspects of the operation. The architect may provide and supervise (upon request of the school board) the installation of furniture and movable equipment. The school board must decide if it wants the architect to provide the furnishings (if they do, they must pay a percentage fee for the selection activity). The school board may elect to contract for many of these furnishings themselves. Sub-contracting for heating, plumbing, and related activities should normally be supervised by the architect.

In most school building projects, the school board is quite dependent on the architect, and it is very important that the superintendent and school board be kept informed on the progress of the building. The architect's personal assurance of the progress of the building to the school board will serve to create a relationship which helps the entire construction process.

As the project nears completion, a semi-final inspection is made by the architect and the contractors. Usually a list of items to be completed is prepared and used as a master list to make sure all final corrections are made by the contractor. Final inspection is made by the architect, and if all requirements are met, he or she recommends final acceptance of the project to the school board. The final payment certificate is approved by the architect.

The post-completion service of the architect has become increasingly important. Usually, a complete inspection is made within a year after completion to see if any further work is needed by the contractor in accordance with guarantees provided.

In order to insure the proper functioning of the building after completion, the school board should appoint the building custodian before completion. A thorough knowledge of the building, service systems, and other components is essential for a smooth transition to actual operation. This early assignment will usually result in more efficient use and maintenance of the building.

The Contractor

Probably the most important task of the contractor in a school building project is the adherence to a time schedule. Most school buildings are timed to open at the beginning of a school term, and there is very seldom any leeway for attaining this goal. The contractor or his or her representative, usually referred to as a superintendent, must provide continuous supervision on the job. This superintendent must work very closely with the architect to be sure that all requirements are being met. If sub-contractors are used, diligent coordination by the contractor will be necessary. The timing and the expediting of sub-contract work is usually one of the contractor's most difficult tasks.

The contractor must continuously maintain adequate protection of all his or her work and should protect the owner's property from injury or loss arising in connection with the contract. He or she must also make good on damage or losses that are due to his or her negligence.

The contractor must submit to the architect evidence that all bills, liens, etc., have been met before requesting monthly payments from the school district.

Key Points

1. An educator does not translate the educational requirements or specifications into architectural specifications or drawings. Knowing how the educational specifications may be used, however, can assist in an understanding of the relevance of the "ed specs."
2. An architect performs a wide range of services for the school board beyond developing "drawings."
3. Flexibility, a key to future curriculum change, is permitted in a

new facility by careful design and placement of load-bearing walls, air ducts, plumbing, electrical connections, conduits for communications, window placement, and so on.
4. "Systems Buildings" are modular buildings which can reduce construction cost and time requirements.
5. Windowless classrooms can reduce construction, maintenance, and heating and air conditioning costs. They can keep distractions from entering the classroom.
6. Construction supervision is a critical task performed by the architect.

Notes

1. Educational Facilities Laboratories. *Planning for Higher Education.* New York: Educational Facilities Laboratories, Inc., 1972.

2. Detroit Public Schools. *New Tactics for Building.* Detroit: Detroit Public Schools, January, 1975.

3. Larson, C.T. *The Effect of Windowless Classrooms on Elementary School Children.* University of Michigan: College of Architecture and Design, 1966, p. 33.

4. *Ibid.,* p. 33.

5. *Ibid.,* p. 44.

6. *Ibid.,* pp. 51-52.

Chapter Four

Site Planning and Development for New Facilities

After a school board has decided it needs a new facility, and after the educational program has been determined, and usually after an architect has been engaged, a site for the school must be obtained and developed. Site selection may be started before an architect is selected but should not be finalized until the architect has been hired.

The architect can assist in site evaluation by examining test borings of the land and drainage conditions to insure the site is suitable for buildings, playgrounds, and access. He or she should examine the possible utility connections and suggest ways to take advantage of the natural growth, surrounding buildings, and topographic features. The school district may contract with the architect to aid in the landscaping of a site, or it may make arrangements to pay the architect a fee for expenses related to the site selection service.

Site Planning

The site may be a new one requiring the purchase of additional land, or it may be one already owned by the board. The site selection should be based on trade-offs of these considerations:

1. Is the site centrally located with reference to the using children?
2. Is the site large enough, and of such a shape that it will accommodate the building(s), outdoor recreation, bus loading, parking (300 square feet, or 28 square meters, per vehicle) for staff, visitors, students, and future expansion?
3. Is the site well removed from distracting noises, unpleasant odors, and pollution?
4. Is the site located away from hazards, such as main roads, railroads, or high tension electric lines, near which the children may have to walk?
5. Is the site located so that sewage, water, electricity, and other utilities can be inexpensively obtained?
6. Does the site have good elevation and contour, insuring drainage?
7. Will the subsoil provide a good base for building footings and foundations (this can be determined by borings)?
8. Does the site have at least one good access?
9. How is the surrounding land zoned? Will this area as it is developed enhance the school? Can the site be expanded in the future?
10. Is the site aesthetically pleasing and easy to landscape?
11. Is the site accessible for adult, summer, or evening programs?
12. Is the site affordable?

Elementary school sites should also include spaces for supervised or organized games and for free-play activities. *Junior high school* sites should permit track, softball, soccer, volleyball, or football. *Senior high schools* may have basketball, baseball, tennis, track, football, volleyball, archery, and softball areas. Driver training and nature study areas may also be desired.

A rule-of-thumb for minimum site size in suburban and rural

school areas is that an elementary school should have at least seven acres (28,000 square meters) plus one acre per each 100 pupils. A junior high (middle) school (7-8 or 7-9) should have 15 acres (61,000 square meters) plus one acre for every 100 pupils. A senior high school should have 20 acres (81,000 square meters) plus one acre for every 100 anticipated pupils. Due to the premium placed on land in the cities, high-rise buildings or multiple-use dwellings with little playground, bus parking, automobile parking, or landscaped area may, of necessity, be adequate.

School size determines the accessibility of a school. A number of small "neighborhood" schools are usually more accessible than a few large, centrally situated schools. An elementary school child can be expected to walk a half to three-quarters of a mile, and high school students can walk one to two miles. While small schools are more convenient, they tend to be a little more costly on a per pupil basis.

Possible sites may be located by studying a map and driving through the area where the school is desired. The site may be identified by examining the comprehensive community plan, if one exists. In this way, the professional community planning people can be used and the zoning and future growth of the community considered. Aerial photographs, topographic maps, highway maps, attendance, or other school published maps or information may be useful in identifying possible sites. The criteria discussed above apply to all sites. A comparison of alternative potential sites may be made by giving each factor a weight, as shown in Figure 4.1.

In the example, the size of the site was considered more important than the ease of site acquisition and thus received a higher possible score. Each school system will want to develop its own relative weights to reflect their values. A district, for example, may wish to value the size of a site more than the 16 in this illustration. The relative cost of the land is assumed, in this illustration, to be fair and is not included. It might be added to some weighted lists. In the above illustration, the Able site is the most desirable school site.

Figure 4.1

Site Scoring Form

Item	Maximum Points Allowable	Able Site	Baker Site	Charlie Site	Delta Site
Size and Ease of Future Expansion	16	16	13	16	14
Location to Student Population	14	14	10	6	8
Accessibility	13	12	11	3	12
Soil	12	11	11	11	11
Topography	10	9	8	6	7
Environment	11	10	9	11	11
Utilities (Availability and Cost)	7	6	6	3	5
Ease of Acquisition	7	6	5	5	4
Cost	10	10	9	7	7

Following the selection of a site, an appraisal of the property should be made. Some school administrators advocate using a realtor, or other disinterested party, to negotiate for the board. This is sometimes done, since some property owners tend to raise prices when they discover public monies are involved. If negotiations fail to produce an agreement, the board of education may have to exercise its "right of eminent domain" by instituting condemnation proceedings through the courts. State laws should be examined when acquiring land, as various states require state department of education approval, and other states have limitations on negotiating for school properties.

A title search should be done and be as fully guaranteed as possible. This procedure is particularly important in urban areas, where the purchase of a school site may involve many lot-sized parcels of land.

Site Development

If the school is an urban school, the school board should consult with the city planning board and urban planners to determine the best way(s) to integrate the school with the community. This contact should be made during the site acquisition process to make best use of population shift data and other available information.

A landscape architect, possibly part of the general architect's service, should be engaged to prepare a master plan for the site development. Walks should be located along "natural" paths—do not pave sidewalks which will not be used by the students. A landscape architect at Michigan State University reportedly pours school walks only after the students have *worn a path.* He then knows the walks reflect the actual, and practical, pattern desired by the students.

Decorative and functional grading should improve the appearance of the school facility and screen it from noise which would distract learners.

Safety and accessibility are extremely important. All roads or walkways should be laid out to prevent foot traffic and vehicle traffic from crossing any more than is absolutely necessary. The general architect or landscape architect should prepare a site development plan to show these safety-related considerations.

Key Points

1. There are many considerations which must be weighed when identifying possible school sites and when selecting the best site. A site scoring form can be used to make the decisions more objective.
2. Safety and accessibility are among the major considerations in choosing a site for a new school.

Chapter Five

Costs and Funding
of New Facilities

An analysis of building budgets for all types of schools suggests the approximate cost breakdown for new schools as shown in Figure 5.1. This breakdown will vary some for any given building due to the cost of the site, the type of building, the services sought from the architect and other consultants, the bonding costs, etc. Your architect can provide refined figures for your area and/or project(s).

Besides the initial cost of designing and constructing a school, there are other factors which must be considered in determining the cost-effectiveness of a building. Anything which handicaps the educational program, reduces the safety, or increases maintenance or insurance costs quickly outweighs initial potential "savings." Efficiency in school plant construction is a complex relationship between original cost, maintenance, and operating expense, and—of most importance—*educational productivity*. Will the new building make it more probable that effective and efficient learning will take place?

Economy in school facilities design requires:

(1) the determination of the functions and size of the required facility;

Figure 5.1

Cost Categories for New Buildings

Surveys and Consultants		1%
Bonding		1%
Site Costs		10%
Landscaping and Development		7%
Architects and Engineers		7%
Construction		65%
General	40 to 52%	
Heating/Cooling	6 to 11%	
Plumbing	4 to 6%	
Electrical	3 to 8%	
Equipment and Furnishings (movable)		7%
Miscellaneous		2%
	Total	100%

---

(2) the quality of the building and fixtures;

(3) the ability to pay for the facility;

(4) a forecast of future needs; and

(5) sound judgment in balancing the four previous factors.

Economy, as related to educational facilities, cannot be measured by using the cost per square foot of the building as the sole measure for making an evaluation. It's what's inside that counts— how productively educational functions are permitted, contrasted with alternative ways of getting the same jobs accomplished.

The following is a list of considerations which may reduce the cost of a new educational facility:

1. Design the building for high utilization by having as much space as possible serve several functions—design flexible space.

2. Design the building for minimum, but adequate, ventilation. See Chapter Six.

3. Choose construction materials for durability and easy maintenance.

4. Design buildings with a minimum of, or no, glass to reduce maintenance, construction costs, heat gain from sunlight, heat loss, and to increase internal flexibility and light control.
5. Design the building around modular and/or prefabricated units—interior and exterior. Considerable time may also be saved. See Chapter Three.
6. Consider the use of carpeting as a method for economically obtaining acoustical control and flooring.
7. Survey the costs of the various fuels in your area and select the least expensive (also figure the cost of the heating system and its maintenance).
8. If land is expensive, multiple-story buildings will usually be less expensive per square foot; otherwise, single-story buildings will usually be less expensive.
9. Keep the exterior perimeter walls to a minimum. If air conditioning is not to be used, increasing the exterior wall space to increase ventilation may be a desirable trade-off.
10. Plan the most efficient arrangement of spaces. Keep the ratio of gross square footage to usable square footage as low as possible. Corridor spaces are expensive. Round buildings tend to reduce corridors.
11. Bidding should be related to seasonal factors and local conditions. Construction is a cyclic business with peak activity in the spring and summer.
12. Participate in a systems approach to building when possible. The creation of a consortium of schools to create a guaranteed market through the design of compatible components and common specifications will reduce square footage costs by reducing the design and special construction problems.

Windowless, compact schools offer more efficient use of space with lower construction and operating costs.[1,2] The cost of energy, however, to run the ventilation system and/or the air conditioning will reduce the cost advantage of these compact buildings.

The architect makes cost estimates on the basis of preliminary drawings prior to the beginning of the school bond issue vote. The actual cost of construction is not known until the bids are opened. This occurs after the passage of the school bond issue vote (if all goes well). The cost of learning space is rapidly rising. Thus, build today—not tomorrow—if you *need* the facilities now.

As an architect's fees are usually based on a percentage of the total building costs, the use of "stock plans" will not result in savings for the school district.

The school construction dollar is divided roughly into three parts. Over one-third goes for materials, about one-third is for on-site labor costs, and less than one-third usually goes for off-site labor costs.

Joint Occupancy Buildings

An alternative way to fund school buildings has been found in New York State through the "Garrison Law" passed in 1966. New York City established the New York Educational Construction Fund, which can issue its own bonds to cover construction costs of a project and then retire those bonds out of the income it receives from "joint occupancy" buildings.

An example of joint occupancy is P.S. 126 in New York City. This project is partly an elementary school for 1,200 children and partly a 400-apartment complex for middle-income residents in the Bronx. The residents' rent pays the interest and the principal on the bonds. The city, thus, gets a very low-cost school. The apartment dwellers get the use of the "school's" recreational facilities in the evenings and on weekends. P.S. 169 in Manhattan is another joint use facility.[3]

A private school in Philadelphia entered into an agreement with a large chemical firm which rents space at about $200,000 per year. This income is more than enough to cover the interest and debt retirement costs of the bonds on the buildings.

It is possible in a high-rise joint occupancy building having either apartments or office spaces to expand or contract the size of the "school" as the school population expands or contracts. This can be done by going up or down a floor. Some of the year-long leases would not be renewed and some of the internal walls would be taken out to make room for the classrooms. The elevator banks would be split and even the entrances to the elevators can be located off different streets so there would normally be little contact between the students and the joint-use occupants. The elevators would be "locked" so they would only stop at the appropriate floors. There are many possibilities in this alternative way of funding school facilities. (See Figure 5.2.)

Competitive Bids and Construction

After the educational and architectural specifications have been translated into preliminary plans and developed to the satisfaction of the board of education, they must be converted into a building. This can be done only after the money is voted (or otherwise made available). Then the final detailed drawings must be made, the competitive bidding accomplished, and the construction begun.

Competitive bidding is usually required by state law. The lowest bidder normally obtains the award. Frequently, the bidders must give some assurance that they will accept the bid if it is offered to them. This assurance may be the depositing of a certified check or the filing of a bid bond.

Contract awards may be made when the bids are opened. Occasionally, questions concerning the responsibility and reliability of the lower bidder may result in a higher bid being selected. The construction contracts should be clear as to (1) the work performed, (2) the guarantees to be provided, (3) the bond to be required, (4) the completion date and penalties (if any), and (5) the payment schedule.

Acceptance of the building should occur only after the building is completed. The architect will issue a certificate of final

Figure 5.2

Joint Occupancy Building

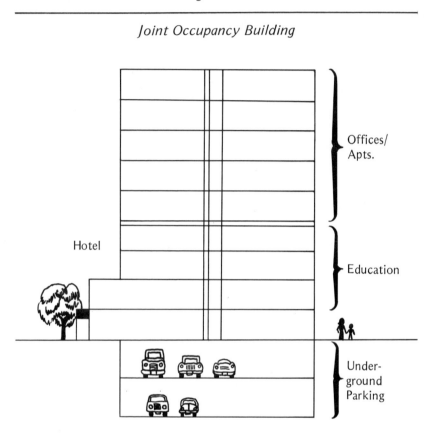

approval, which should be signed by the board after a complete firsthand inspection. If some aspects of the work are unfinished, or need correcting, a percentage of the balance should be withheld until the work has been completed. The architect and the board of education should then sign a "Certificate of Completion and Acceptance of the Building."

The building is now finished and ready for final furnishing and occupancy, following approval by local and building inspectors and state education agencies.

Key Points

1. Estimates of the cost of a new facility can be fairly accurate if the planning is adequately done.
2. While the form of the building should be dictated by the functions or activities the building is to house, there are many trade-offs which an instructional designer can make to reduce the initial cost and the later maintenance and operational expenses.
3. Joint occupancy buildings have been used successfully to reduce the capital expenditure for new facilities in states where supporting legislation has been enacted.
4. Once the money has been voted for the new facilities, the architect must complete the final detailed drawings, and then competitive bidding can be accomplished for the construction.

Notes

1. Blair, W.G. "Compact School and $$ Savings." *American School Board Journal,* May, 1966, pp. 32-33.

2. Berlowitz, Manfred, Drucker, Eugene, and Scarbrough, William. *Thermal Environment of Educational Facilities.* Albany, N.Y.: Division of Educational Facilities Planning, State Education Department, 1969.

3. Meier, James. *Combined Occupancy Development.* New York: Educational Facilities Laboratories, Inc., 1971.

Chapter Six

The Thermal Environment

Temperature, relative humidity, air movement, odor, and air cleanliness are important when providing a comfortable environment for learning. The human organism is highly adaptive, but a student cannot attend, perceive, or process information easily when his or her physical environment is uncomfortable.

In a working paper funded by the U.S. Office of Education, George D. Greer identified some tolerance limits for heat, assuming that persons are dressed optimally for the conditions. Because students do not have the opportunity to modify their dress to a range of temperatures, his temperature figures are not useful here, but his rule-of-thumb for performance *is*: "... performance begins to deteriorate for any given condition at about 75 percent of the physiological tolerance limit. It is possible, however, to exceed these values for short periods of time through adaptation, and habitation, or through high motivation."[1] A good teaching situation may overcome some of the hot classrooms in the spring, summer, or fall, but as often as not, students may have to struggle simply to keep awake and look like they are participating. Greer also bemoans the fact that there is a striking lack of solid research on the effects of temperature on higher mental processes.

Evaluation of student or teacher performance by relating a specific stimulus with a given response is difficult. Thus, statements relating cognitive or affective gains to temperature, lighting, or other environmental conditions are difficult to make with any degree of certainty. Simulation facilities which control many of the extraneous stimuli are fairly expensive to construct and program. NASA has done so, but their focus has been oriented toward "getting a man on the moon," not on educational tasks.

Individual metabolic rates are different and will affect an "ideal" classroom temperature. Men often prefer a temperature a couple of degrees below that preferred by women. Elementary and secondary students generally prefer a somewhat cooler area than do adults. Specific data involving temperatures for various learner activities are not readily available. Air temperatures of 68° to 70°F, 30 inches above the floor (20° to 21°C at 76 cm) for primary grade students engaged in sedentary classroom activities and temperatures of 68° to 74°F, 30 inches above the floor (20° to 23°C at 76 cm) for older students seem to be both healthful and comfortable during the heating season. The difference in temperature between the floor and the temperature at the five-foot level should not vary by more than 3°F (2°C).

A temperature range between 60° to 70°F (15° to 21°C) for vigorous activities will usually be comfortable. As the planned physical activity becomes more vigorous, the temperature should decrease toward the 60°F (15°C) level. An exception to this is the swimming pool area, where an air temperature of just over 80°F (27°C) with water temperature above 75°F (24°C) is comfortable. A temperature of over 75°F (24°C) is comfortable in the locker room area.

The American Society of Heating, Refrigerating, and Air Conditioning Engineers' charts (*ASHRAE Handbook of Fundamentals*) show that for men and women at rest in normal winter clothing, the optimum temperature is 67.5°F (19.7°C) with a range from 65° to 70°F (18° to 21°C). In the summer, it is 71°F (22°C) with a range from 68° to 73°F (20° to 22°C). The best temperatures for children, they suggest, are difficult to determine but are likely to be one or two degrees lower. The activity the child is involved in modifies his or her optimum surrounding temperature requirements. If he or she is active, a cooler temperature is required. With energy conservation programs, it may be necessary to raise the summer upper limit to 78°F (26°C) or even 80°F (27°C).

John W. Gilliand reported a study involving over 10,000 temperature readings taken from classrooms which suggests that 44 percent of all classroom temperatures were above 75°F (24°C). Only two percent of the classrooms were below 70°F (21°C).[2]

When an environment is too warm for an individual, there is evidence to suggest that the ability to perform certain tasks deteriorates.[3,4] An over-heated child often ceases to concentrate on academic matters and relaxes into daydreams. Dr. Gilliand suggests that for every degree of room temperature rise above the optimum level, a student's learning ability may be reduced by two percent.

The *relative humidity* of learning spaces influences student comfort. A relative humidity range of 40 to 60 percent is usually considered comfortable. At temperatures of about 70°F (21°C), a 60 percent relative humidity level is comfortable. As the temperature rises, however, the relative humidity should decrease if comfort is to be maintained.

The translation of these educational specifications into architectural designs is more straightforward than in other areas. Limiting the temperature range virtually requires air conditioning. The efficient use of air conditioning suggests a compact school design, such as an open plan or a loft plan school, as opposed to a corridor plan, finger plan, or courtyard plan school. Since natural ventilation is not a concern, but heat loss or gain is, a large windowed exterior area is not desired.

Schools should be designed for temperature control by incorporating design principles involving minimum window surfaces, the use of draperies or similar window covering, and by taking the building orientation into design consideration. If the school is designed so that it interferes with the effectiveness of student (or teacher) activities, the main purpose of the building is negated.

Schools can be designed for efficient temperature control by following one or more of the following design principles: (1) the orientation or placement of the building, (2) building mass, (3) lighting reduction to include minimizing exterior windows, and (4) the collection and storage of inexpensive energy.

Orient the building to receive the maximum amount of sun in the cold months and the minimum in the summer. (See Figure 6.1.) The use of deciduous trees on the south side of the building may be used to shade the building in the summer; and when the leaves fall in the winter, the sun can get to the building to assist in its heating.

If windows are desired, orient the school building to control the light as well as the direct heat from the sunlight on the building. Overhangs on the south will protect the learning spaces in the spring, summer, and fall from intense heat and light. In the winter, when the sun is lower to the southern horizon, the light and heat can get below the overhang. The heat of the afternoon sun makes the use of overhangs or window "shades" or blinds necessary on the western side of the building. Trees may be used to assist in the shading of the window and wall areas. The weak north light is the most desirable from a learning specification standpoint. Coniferous trees on the north side of the building can be used as a windbreak from the colder north winds.

The second way to design a building for efficient temperature control is by increasing the building mass and by making the envelope of the educational activities more efficient. A building which is nearly square has a large central mass. A school using a "finger plan" or one that has a large amount of exterior wall space will transmit much desired interior heat (or cooling) through the exterior walls to the outside, and the energy used in heating (or

Figure 6.1

Building Orientation

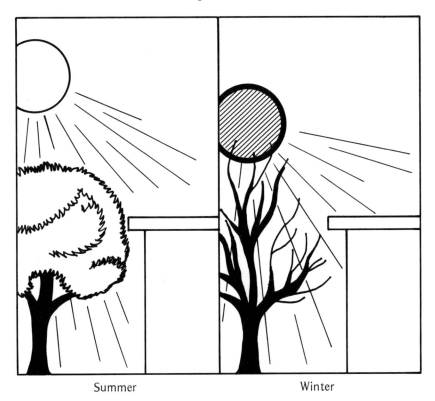

| Summer | Winter |

---

cooling) that space will be wasted. The greater the temperature differential between the desired inside temperature and the outside temperature, the bigger the problem. Insulation should be generously used to reduce this heat transfer. If body heat in the school generates a problem, then increase the ventilation, if the outside air is cool. If possible, use this heat by pumping it into a heat storage "tank." Use silver or white colors on the roof to reflect light and heat from the school and reduce heat transfer. The design of underground schools can substantially affect the heat transfer. A buried building will maintain a constant temperature somewhat lower than that normally desired for schools. The heat from the students, lights, and motors is usually enough to offset this effect. The earth acts as an excellent insulator. A well-designed underground building can be beautiful, comfortable, and efficient. (See Figure 6.2.)

The third principle for controlling temperature is to operate with minimum acceptable lighting. The more lighting required in the school, the more heat that's generated by the lighting fixtures.

The fourth way of designing school buildings to efficiently control temperature is by collecting and storing inexpensive energy. Energy can be inexpensively collected from solar sources, wind, student body heat, and possibly from water. This energy may be transferred by heat pumps into water or rock storage areas. Many of these techniques are somewhat experimental at this time but should be considered whenever building a new school.

The traditional approach of using the wind to blow air through open windows is great when it works. In many cases, especially if your energy costs are high, you will want to consider this approach. These "finger plan" schools create problems with regard to site selection and floor plan design to "capture" the wind, and they restrict the flexibility of the space because moving the interior walls and learning spaces might block the air flow.

Air Conditioning

Educational Facilities Laboratories has published a number of studies on schools which have used air conditioning. In a report on the Bel Air Senior High School, they suggested the following benefits could be gained from air conditioning:

(1) ideal indoor climate (temperature, humidity, dust, and pollen) for learning and good health;

(2) flexibility and adaptability of classroom size and space;

(3) stability of teaching-learning efficiency year-round;

(4) better control of light and sound for instructional media teaching techniques; and

Figure 6.2

Underground School

Photo Credit: Allen and Miller Architects. Freemont Elementary School, Santa Ana Unified School District, California.

---

(5) better control of noise generating activities.

A report supported by the New York State Education Department states, "The school of the near future will be a compact, completely air conditioned building with a minimum of glass surface."[5]

One of the earliest studies examining the effects of air conditioning was accomplished at the University of Iowa in 1962.[6] Charles Peccolo used a specially built two-room research school in which he established "ideal" conditions (70-74°F temperature, 40-60 percent relative humidity, and 20-40 feet per minute air motion) in one room. The other room was left without air conditioning. In it, the temperature varied from 72 to 80°F

(21° to 27°C), the relative humidity ranged from 33 to 75 percent, and the air motion was from five to ten feet per minute. The teacher could open windows and adjust a thermostat. Forty-four matched pairs of fourth graders were used in the study. After three weeks, the students in the air conditioned room displayed greater progress (completion of mazes, solving math problems, reasoning tasks, clerical tasks) than their less comfortable counterparts.

At Kansas State University, 72 college students subjected to controlled temperatures ranging in six degree increments from 62° to 92°F (17° to 33°C) learned more easily (time to complete assignment and effort required—subjective) and with a minimum error rate at 80°F (27°C) (relative humidity was constant at 45 percent).[7]

Willard R. Lane conducted a study in 1966 entitled, "Thermal Environment and Learning" (see note No. 5, cited earlier). In this study, 44 matched pairs of fourth grade students were divided into two equal groups and ranked according to achievement measured on the Iowa Test of Basic Skills. The experimental group was placed into an environment suggested as ideal, i.e., air conditioned. The results indicated:

(1) the reasoning activity of the boys and girls in the experimental environment improved significantly beyond the students in the control group;

(2) the clerical and routine task results favored the experimental group, but not statistically; and

(3) the measurements related to the development of new concepts between the groups was not significantly different, but the students designated as high achievers performed better under the controlled thermal conditions in nine out of ten tasks, while low level students in the model environment surpassed the performance level students in the non-controlled thermal environment in eight out of ten tasks.

Robert McCardle conducted a study in a two-classroom building where he could control the thermal environment.[8] One classroom was an air conditioned environment and the other classroom was not. Forty matched pairs of sixth grade students were selected and taught by instructional materials to eliminate the teacher variable. He found that the students made significantly fewer errors and took less time in the air conditioned room.

The above studies provide some direction concerning "ideal temperatures," but they do not seem to support each other as well as they might. Further work is needed on the question, "what temperatures (or ranges) do students engaged in various activities require to operate most effectively?"

A student's psychological reaction to color will influence his or her perception of warmth and coolness. Red, yellow, or orange colors may "warm up" a room having a northern exposure, and grey, blue, or green may relax and give a feeling of coolness. The selection of colors should be determined in conjunction with the educational and architectural specifications.

Heating

In most areas of the United States, the heat given off from electric incandescent lights, appliances, audio-visual media, and by teacher and student body heat is sufficient to heat a building when the school is in session. Each student's metabolic process generates so much heat (200 to 600 British Thermal Units per hour, about the equivalent of a 100 watt bulb each) that a New York City heating consultant ran an experiment in Moline, Illinois in the winter.[9] He found that the classrooms needed heat from 7:00 to 8:30 A.M. and again from 12:00 to 1:00 P.M. The rest of the day, heat had to be removed from the classrooms.

The amount of heat produced by an individual will vary according to age and activity. For a quietly seated seven-year-old, the hourly heat production is about 200 British Thermal Units per hour (BTU/hr.). An average adult produces about 400 BTU/hr. sitting, 600 BTU/hr. standing, and from 1,000-2,000 BTU/hr. with light to moderate activity. To make clear the amount of energy dissipated as heat by people, it should be noted that 30 teenage pupils doing class work probably produce about 15,000 BTU/hr., which is 15 percent to 25 percent of the heat released by an average residential furnace.[10] This body heat, if used in conjunction with a heat exchange system, can drastically reduce or eliminate the need for a heat system. These figures indicate how important an air flow or an air conditioning system is in warm weather.

The lights for a 1,000-square foot classroom with a 50-foot-candle light level adds about 7,500 BTUs to the room. The major winter problem concerning school heating in most climates is not really of providing heat for the buildings but is rather of how to control the heat so that pollution and undesirable odors are removed from the air. The fresh air, if it is heated, may have to be humidified in the winter to be within desired limits. A ventilation system providing at least ten cubic feet of fresh air per student is adequate for the distribution of fresh air and for the removal of carbon dioxide, dust, pollen, bacteria, and odors. Many states have codes requiring up to 30 cubic feet per student per minute. The air motion should not have a velocity of more than 25 feet per minute, or drafts and noise levels will result. Furnishings and movable partitions will affect air motion and should be considered in the architectural specifications.

There are several different *heating systems.* Each system has features which make it best suited to particular situations. In smaller educational facilities, as in many small elementary schools, forced hot air or hot water or low pressure steam systems may be used. In larger schools, such as secondary schools having a capacity of 1,000 or more students, either a low pressure steam system or a hot water system may be used to heat the school. In extremely large or physically separate facilities, such as college campuses served by a central power plant, a high pressure steam system is likely to be the best distribution system. *Heat pumps,* which cool buildings in the summer and are "reversed" in action to provide heat in the winter, are now seeing some use, but only where the winters are not very severe.

Any of the above heating systems may be used in conjunction with a *radiant heat* distribution system. This radiant heat system consists of a system of pipes, usually embedded in a floor or ceiling of the area being heated. When hot water is pumped through the pipes in the floors, it is more comfortable for the children to sit on the floor or to have activities on or near the floor.

Energy Considerations

A favorite *fuel* for schools today is oil. Each grade dictates its own heating plant. The cheapest grade of fuel (which pollutes the outside air with sulfur compounds) requires the most expensive heating plant and maintenance.

Coal will become a much more widely used fuel in schools, despite the storage and ash removal problems. As petroleum products become increasingly expensive, coal must become the fuel of choice.

One way of beating the high cost of energy is to insulate buildings well. Between ten percent to 35 percent of heating or cooling costs could reasonably be expected to be saved by insulation. Clark County School District, Nevada, insulated one of its schools and they found the cost for the insulation was paid for almost immediately.[11]

Windows are the greatest villains in the heat loss, and thus energy loss, category. Windows permit a lot of heat transfer from inside the building to the outside and vice versa. Windows, if they must be included in the plant design, should be insulated and used sparingly. Believing this, the people in Mapleton, Minnesota decided to retrofit their aging buildings by installing insulated panels for their old windows. The panel is constructed of aluminum with a urethane core and has an R factor of six to eight, as compared to the one for glass.[12] Insulation materials for walls and ceilings usually range between 12 and 19. The higher the R value, the better the insulator, and the less the loss or transfer.

This same community, when designing a new gymnasium, decided to build it without windows, as they concluded that electricity for lights would cost less than replacing heat lost through the windows.

Another example of energy reduction occurred in the Terraset Elementary School in Reston, Virginia. They saved 50 percent of the conventional heating costs by building into a hill and using the dirt as insulation. Reston administrators also installed a heat reclamation system to keep heat given off by people, machines, and lights from being lost.[13] Underground schools will become more popular as the cost of energy increases.

Another way to obtain low cost energy is to use solar power. The school board in Florida, N.Y., installed a solar heating system for $80,000 and projects savings of 35 percent in their fuel costs.[14] At current fuel prices, the entire cost of their solar heating system will be returned in under ten years. The new north campus of the Community College of Denver also uses solar energy. They spent 1.1 million dollars on the solar heating system, or 8.5 percent of the total construction cost. They expect to recover this expenditure in 11 years.[15] The National Solar Heating and Cooling Information Center (P.O. Box 1607, Rockville, Maryland 20850), a United States Department of Energy supported organization which disseminates information on solar energy, will provide a list of schools using solar systems which can provide current and additional information. (See Figure 6.3.)

Energy use in schools is high, in part, because vast quantities of air must either be heated or cooled to comply with state and local codes for ventilation. The percentage of outdoor air required for schools seems to have been arbitrarily set. Local codes may have to be amended to permit reduced minimum percentages of outdoor air. The modification of codes would, by itself, account for a substantial savings in energy and thus operating costs.

Ideally, a ventilation system should be flexible enough to use 100 percent outside air when temperatures are appropriate, or it should permit going to a minimum of ten percent outdoor air when the outside temperature and humidity dictate this mix.

Figure 6.3

Solar Energy Heated School

Photo Credit: AAI Corporation. Timonium Elementary School, Maryland.

Another source of heat energy, seldom used to heat schools but planned for in the design of many commercial buildings, is found in the heat given off by the lighting system.

Summary

In summary, due to the increasing cost of energy, the desirability of a compact, windowless school, designed to permit the best possible temperature and humidity levels, should be continually studied. The use of solar energy and insulation will affect the cost of heating and cooling. A study by the architect of needs and geography may be desirable to determine what general type of air control system will be most advantageous.

Key Points

1. Learning is enhanced when the temperature, relative humidity, air movement, odor, and air cleanliness are within limits acceptable to the learner.
2. The decision of whether or not to use air conditioning will dictate the general type of building. Compact buildings should be designed when air conditioning is used; and designs which permit a maximum of outside air to enter, such as the "finger plan," should be used when air conditioning is not used.
3. The orientation of the building can reduce or complicate the heating and cooling problems. Constructing a school so that it is underground results in an excellent shelter and requires very little additional insulation, as the earth is an excellent insulator.
4. Cooling a building is much more important in planning than is heating due to the heat generated by students and electrical appliances.
5. The cost of energy is resulting in many new approaches to generating heat and electricity. Careful attention must be given to the type of fuel used, the type of heating or cooling plant, and the amount of insulation in the building.

Notes

1. Greer, George D. *et al.* "An Examination of Four Major Factors Impacting on Psychomotor Performance Effectiveness." A working paper for the Special Media Institute, Psychomotor Conference, Teaching Research, Monmouth, Oregon, January, 1970.

2. *Environmental Learning.* University of Tennessee: School Planning Laboratory, 1968.

3. Harmon, Darell. *Controlling the Thermal Environment of the Coordinated Classroom.* Minneapolis Honeywell Corp., 1953.

4. Lane, W.R. *Thermal Environment and Learning.* University of Iowa: Iowa Center for Research in School Administration, 1966.

5. Berlowitz, Manfred, Drucker, Eugene, and Scarbrough, William. *Thermal Environment of Educational Facilities.* Albany, N.Y.: Division of Educational Facilities Planning, State Education Department, 1969.

6. *Air Conditioning for Schools.* New York: Educational Facilities Laboratories, Inc., March, 1971, p. 6.

7. *Ibid.,* p. 7.

8. McCardle, Robert. "Thermal Environment and Learning." Unpublished doctoral dissertation, University of Iowa, 1966.

9. Wright, Henry. "Classroom Heating and Ventilating." *American School and University,* Vol. 23, 1951-52, pp. 197-216.

10. Berlowitz, *op. cit.,* p. 11.

11. Bokelmann, S.O. "Savings Can Pay the Cost of Insulation." *American School and University,* July, 1977, pp. 24-25.

12. Mordue, Dale, and Ward, Douglas. "How One School District Avoided Burning Up Dollars." *Phi Delta Kappan,* October, 1977, p. 130.

13. Downey, Gregg. "Solar Energy Schools May Not Be as Far Off or as Blue Sky as We've Thought." *The American School Board Journal,* August, 1977, pp. 56-60.

14. Downey, *op. cit.*

15. *Chronicle of Higher Education,* May 2, 1977, p. 3.

Chapter Seven

Acoustical Control

Effects of Noise on Learning

The psychological and physical health of the students and staff are important to school planners. The physical plant must be stimulating to the learners and should ease teaching-learning tasks. Facilities planning should take into consideration all those design features which affect learning, such as the reduction of undesirable background noise. The more obtrusive the noise and the more complex the learning task, the greater the probability of interference with performance.

Predicting the effects of noise or of sound levels on a given student is difficult due to the duration and spectral composition of sound. Noise tolerance levels vary from person to person. Generally, hearing-related problems or hearing losses result from longer and louder noise (air pressure) levels. Where noise levels exceed 70 decibels—the din of ordinary expressway traffic—it can cause, according to the Environmental Protection Agency, temporary stress reactions, including increased heart rate, blood pressure, and blood cholesterol.

Short-term noise exposure for unprotected ears of 135 decibels may cause physiological effects, such as nausea, fatigue, and a loss of muscular coordination.

Low-intensity background noise may simply be annoying and result in distraction from desired learning tasks. When audio stimuli are desired by the instructional designer, the threshold for hearing these stimuli goes up as the background noise level rises. This "masking effect" by the background noise is greatest when the frequency range of the desired audio stimuli and the background noise are similar. It is for this reason that a teacher or a student's voice in an adjacent learning area causes more problems than the constant hum of a ventilating system. Loud or unexpected sounds in any frequency range will be distracting.

An instructional designer, when considering alternative instructional spaces, will find that the effect of background noises on cognitive and psychomotor performances are not necessarily undesirable. Some common noises mask unexpected sounds and thus prevent disturbing noises from interfering with learning tasks. Some rhythmical and expected sounds, such as "background music," not only mask out unexpected noises and provide privacy, but the rhythm itself may affect learning behaviors. An instructional or systems designer can affect the pacing of a learner in an individualized learning situation. Gradually increasing the rhythm will often increase typing, reading, or other instructional behaviors.

The Muzak Company feels that background music is a tool of contemporary management which improves efficiency and productivity. They conclude that their background music can "induce psychological and physiological effects which will influence the body, the mind, and the emotions both consciously and unconsciously." They suggest that the heart beat, metabolism, and respiration can all be affected by this background music. The "Muzak" has been doctored and processed by their engineers to vary the rhythm, the tempo, and the instrumentation to create effects of increased working efficiency and alertness "by as much as 15 percent."

The ear ranks along with the eye as one of the two major sources of stimulation in the school. The acoustical environment of the school should be of immediate and real concern to educators. Unwanted sounds must be limited. Learners who must strain to hear and participate in their learning may have little energy left with which to learn.

Noise Control

Many classrooms have acoustically hard walls consisting of plaster, tile, or similar building materials which will reflect and sometimes amplify sounds. The use of draperies or acoustical materials, which may also serve as bulletin boards, decorations, and so on, can reduce these unwanted classroom noises. A classroom can be too quiet, however. A classroom should not be any quieter than the quietest room of a home. While the noisy activities of children in another classroom can be disconcerting, so can an acoustically "dead" classroom.

Resistance to open space is often based on a fear of excessive sound, but it appears that there is no demonstrable negative effect beyond violating a personal preference. High pitched and high frequency noises are very disturbing. In order to keep some sounds from disturbing students who are attempting to study, it may be desirable to locate music and other noise-generating activities some distance away from the library and other relatively quiet activities. Another primary source of noise is impact noise which occurs when a book is dropped or a chair tips over.

Noise generated outside the classroom may be reduced by the use of hedges, trees, earth embankments, and masonry walls. While the shrubs and trees might not be very useful in reducing low pitched noises, such as the rumble of a truck, they will reduce the high pitched noises of children playing on the playground. External physical sound barriers should be located as close to the *source* of the noise as possible and not next to the outside walls of the school.

Recent curriculum trends require varying size groups and

activities which, in turn, result in a lot of chair and table movement. A common method of reducing noise involves eliminating the source of irritating and loud sounds. High frequency chair-scraping noises, so common in today's schools with steel legged chairs and hard-surfaced floors, can be eliminated by carpeting. The same carpet, when combined with acoustical ceilings and/or sound-absorbing furnishings in a learning area, may effectively eliminate the need for walls as an acoustical barrier under most conditions.

Corridors are often neglected when it comes to acoustical design. They often can become huge "speaking tubes" in which footsteps and coughs echo. Sound-absorbing materials should be placed in the corridors for the mental and physical health of students and teachers who use them.

Movable partitions can reduce acoustical interference from adjoining instructional areas where team-teaching or other curricular needs require frequent changes in the size of instructional spaces. These partitions, when used in combination with carpeting, can be extremely effective. Acoustical requirements do not necessarily demand floor to ceiling walls; partitions on casters (which may be used to store students' clothing or books, or support the chalkboard or projection screen) may suffice to acoustically insulate teaching stations.

Sound levels are measured in decibels. As a reference, a "quiet" garden may have a 20 decibel level, while the average background noise in a house will, approximately, have a value of 40 decibels. Ordinary conversation will have a 65 decibel level, while the background noise in the street will be about 70 decibels. Each increase of ten decibels actually doubles the apparent noise level.

The acoustical efficiency of a partition is measured technically by the decibels of noise reduced. For example, if a sound at 90 decibels (a scream) hits one side of a partition and a sound at 65 decibels (speech level) can be heard through the partition on the other side, the partition itself has subtracted 25 decibels. This is noise reduction rating of the partition. A background noise level of 45 decibels of sound is acceptable.

The most effective placement of acoustical material can be obtained if acoustical deadening materials are used at the edges of large surfaces or points where two surfaces meet. In other words, the sound-absorbing materials should not be installed, for maximum effectiveness, in the central areas of ceilings. Instead, the edges of the ceilings and the upper walls of the classroom should be treated with acoustical materials.

Undesirable noises originating outside of the building may be controlled by selecting a school site which is removed from the sources of unwanted sounds; suppressing the noise at the source; isolating noisy areas from quiet areas by developing zoned areas; and designing partitions possessing the proper noise reduction characteristics. Glass windows are excellent reflectors of sound.

It is not necessary that educators know the decibel-reducing ratings of various walls, but it is important that they can tell the architect and engineers what activities will be going on in each instructional area and outside of it, and what the educational specifications of that area will require in terms of sound control.

There are at least four major components of "noise" in the classroom. Noise reduction (sound insulation qualities of a barrier); reverberation (liveliness or prolonged reflection of sound); speech interference level (the arithmetic average of background or conflicting noise levels); and the articulation index (ability to recognize speech components).

Audio Amplifier Problems

The use of audio amplifiers with motion picture projectors, tape recorders, or record players results in many problems. The sound level of these projectors is usually greater than speech levels, so more noise reduction is required before the sound reaches adjacent learning areas.

The placement of speakers in large learning areas must be carefully considered so all students have an adequate, but not an excessive, sound level. An acoustical engineer will usually be employed by the architect, if permanent speaker placement is needed.

The Effects of Carpeting

A visit to a school which has carpeting in it will clarify why carpeting is increasingly used in schools. In addition to the acoustical deadening properties, and the attractiveness of it, carpeting permits additional classroom activities. Students often do more work on the floor and there is often more movement in a carpeted classroom. Teachers in carpeted classrooms usually like the carpeting. Many claim they are less fatigued after standing on a carpeted floor all day. Some teachers report that carpeted classrooms seem warmer than non-carpeted rooms.

Summary

Good acoustics in a school results from adequate planning and building designs. A design which hampers communication has failed in fulfilling the purpose of the school plant.

Key Points

1. Unexpected, high frequency noises are especially distracting.
2. Some "background" noise may mask sudden, unexpected high frequencies.
3. Amplified sound from audio-visual equipment is more distracting than a normal voice and requires additional acoustical control.
4. Carpeting and other "acoustical" materials can make large open spaces attractive as teaching-learning areas.

Chapter Eight

Light Control

Effects of Light on Learning

The importance of an appropriate visual environment for learning tasks can hardly be overstated. The light level does make a difference in learning. Measurable productivity changes have been found by simply changing light levels.[1]

The brightness ratio between the visual task and its surroundings is also important. A practical working light ratio of 4 to 1 should not be exceeded. A ratio of 3 to 1 is better. The light on the page of a book, for example, should be no more than four times brighter than the light from the desk top or from the flooring. No part of the study area should be more than five times as bright as the task. Windows and light fixtures should be designed so that light from these sources does not exceed the adaptation capacity of the student's eyes. Intensity and the way light is reflected both affect the brightness level.

Light reflection is measured in foot-lamberts. This measure is used to determine the reflectance of surface areas, not of the light source. See Figure 8.1. When 199 foot-candles of light strikes black velvet material, the velvet "remains quite dark" and absorbs about 95 percent of the light. This lambert reading is about five.

Figure 8.1

Direct and Indirect Light

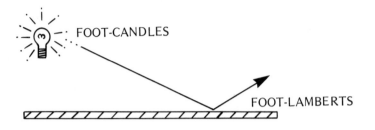

When 100 foot-candles of light strike a light tan tile floor, the floor will appear quite bright because it reflects back about 40 percent of the light. This would mean that an illumination of 60 foot-candles would register 24 foot-lamberts on the meter. Under 60 foot-candles of illumination, a piece of white paper would register 48 foot-lamberts (80 percent reflection). If the student's desk is varnished, problems are created, as almost the full brightness of the light source may be reflected directly into his or her eyes. The task (e.g., book paper) confronting the student should be at least as bright as the surrounding environment. If the task is slightly brighter, this will help the student maintain his or her focus on the work.

Carpeting can be useful in controlling reflection and glare. By providing a low and uniform level of reflection, it avoids the glare problems of a glossy tile floor.

When designing areas which are for media technology use, there are several additional considerations. When films, television, slides, and other visuals are to be viewed in an instructional setting, it is usually undesirable to turn off the overhead lights. The students find it difficult to take notes. The teacher cannot monitor the behavior of the students due to a loss of visual contact with them, so some become mischievous. Complete darkness is not recommended for groups of students viewing A-V materials. A lighting system must be designed so the viewing areas are relatively dark, but the student areas should have some light. Ten foot-candles should suffice.

Demonstration and *chalkboard* areas require much more light than is usually given to them. These areas may be up to 40 feet or more away from the viewers. Seeing the material in these areas requires a high illumination level—up to 150 foot-candles.

In addition to the need for merely sufficient light to see a demonstration, chalkboard, or other wall-mounted visual aid, it is desirable to highlight the desired instructional area. Supermarket, theater, and museum owners have long highlighted the important displays to attract attention to these areas. Educators need to attract attention to the important activity areas in the same way, with the use of highlighting.

Highlighting has been found to increase students' attention as much as 53 percent.[2,3] Attracting the student's attention to the learning task will not assure his or her learning, any more than leading a horse to water will assure the drinking of the water, but getting a student's attention drawn to the learning task through the use of a simple technique like highlighting should not be dismissed.

Study carrels are often under-lit. Because many carrel areas have partitions on three sides, a body on the fourth side, and a head directly over the study area, supplemental lighting is often necessary. An excellent way to light a study carrel is with a straight or U-shaped fluorescent lamp along one or both sides of the carrel. Light along both sides will reduce reflections and thus distracting contrasts in the carrel. It is also desirable to provide carrels with light-colored finishes, resulting in 35 percent or more reflectance. A dark wood grain may produce about ten percent reflectance, while a light wood (like birch) grain finish will provide approximately 35 to 40 percent, and/or a flat white finish will result in 80 to 85 percent reflectance. Because modular ceilings can have light units installed almost anywhere, it is desirable to place them so as to provide the most useful light in the general carrel area. Avoid illumination levels exceeding 70-80 foot-candles in libraries or other learning areas where micro-image readers, television screens, cathode-ray tubes (CRTs), and other projection devices are to be used. The excessive light levels will "wash out" the projected images and they will be unreadable. (See Figure 8.2.)

The efficiency of light fixtures is measured in Equivalent Sphere Illuminance (ESI). ESI is a measure of glare-free illumination. Light fixtures usually attempt to achieve a high ESI. Hanging or surface-mounted fixtures on a white or light glossy colored ceiling can provide a highly efficient lighting system. This arrangement, which uses the ceiling as a light reflector, will also reduce the contrast between the lighting fixture and the ceiling and make a desirable light contrast ratio. Open schools, where the location and size of groupings change, place special problems on the architect, and the selection of lighting systems should be left to him or her.

Light systems which produce many foot-candles and use a great deal of electricity, but do not result in a relatively high ESI, are wasteful. This is especially true if one considers that the majority of the electricity is converted, not into light, but into heat. This heat (except on cold mornings) is undesirable and must be eliminated from the building.

Incandescent vs. Fluorescent Light

While the initial cost of fluorescent fixtures is higher than the cost for incandescent light fixtures, the amount of light produced per kilowatt hour of electricity is almost four times greater for fluorescent lighting. The fluorescent tubes last about 20 times as long. Another cost of operating incandescent bulbs involves the elimination of the heat they generate. Usually the heat is not desired.

A word of caution about fluorescent lights. A study in Sarasota County, Florida, suggests a disturbing link between classroom lighting and hyperactive student behavior. A four-month study, by John Ott, on windowless classrooms, found that hyperactive

Figure 8.2

*Glare Can Make CRT
Screens Unreadable*

students in regular "standard cool white" fluorescent tube lit rooms were more active than hyperactive students in rooms with "improved" fluorescent tubes containing not just the visible light spectrum, but also the long ultraviolet waves. Ott's study was reinforced by one in the Bonny Doon Union School District (Santa Cruz, California). Students moved from fluorescent lit rooms to incandescent lit rooms complained less of headaches and exhibited improved behavior.[4] The quality of light apparently has an impact on the learner.

The light acts on the skin to promote the synthesis of vitamin D. It also acts to control several glands and affects the metabolic processes. The "quality," or spectrum, of light provided thus seems to be very important. The light quality should be equivalent to sunlight found at sea level.[5] General Electric and other bulb manufacturers are developing light sources which can provide this spectrum of light.

Recommendations for specific light levels when instructional media technology is used are provided in Chapter Nine.

Light Levels

As in many other areas of "human factors engineering," there is disagreement on the best light or brightness levels for educational activities. The quantity of light is usually measured in foot-candles. Light ranges or levels have been suggested by *School Lighting* (General Electric) and the *Lighting Handbook* (Illuminating Engineering Society). The light levels in Figure 8.3 will be sufficient for most educational activities. While reading printed material at a desk requires only 30 foot-candles of light, reading pencil writing requires 70 foot-candles, so the recommended lighting for a "standard" desk where reading is to occur has a recommended illumination level of 70 foot-candles. The more detailed the work, in general, the more light is required to perform the task. The glare from the traditional slate blackboard is reduced through the use of painted chalkboards. Few books now have glossy pages or covers. The color and finish of walls, floors, furniture, and ceilings affect the amount of light reflected on a learner. The recommended reflectance ranges for a classroom and for work surfaces are found in Figure 8.4. The lighting sources must be favorably situated to illuminate the room surfaces or the surfaces will appear dark, regardless of their reflectance.

Architects must employ a wide range of window materials and designs in order to bring natural light into a classroom. This is often accomplished in such a manner as to create a feeling of transplanting the classroom to the out-of-doors. The use of natural light may reduce the artificial lighting requirement, and thus, the amount of electricity required to light the school. As has been suggested in an earlier chapter, however, windows in a classroom may also introduce unwanted visual stimuli, undesirable audio

Figure 8.3

Minimum Illumination Levels
for Various Tasks and Locations

	Foot-candles Required
Classrooms	
Reading	70
Art Rooms	70
Drafting Rooms	100
Home Economics, Sewing	150
Home Economics, Cooking	50
Science Laboratories	100
Demonstration Areas	150
Shop Areas	100
Study Halls	70
Typing Rooms	70
Corridors and Stairways	10
Dormitories	
General	10
Reading Area for Books, Magazines	30
Study Desk	70
Cafeterias	
Eating Area	20
Kitchen Area	60
Gymnasiums	
General Exercising Areas	30
Locker and Shower Rooms	30
Exhibition Games	50
Libraries	
Reading Rooms and Carrels	70
Stacks	30

stimuli, and frustrating amounts of heat or cold into the classroom. Windows also permit glare and undesirable brightness contrasts.

Brightness is a basic attribute of a message which is controlled by an instructional designer. An unchanging and homogeneous

Figure 8.4

Reflectance Ranges

sensory field, be it generally light, dark, or colored, becomes perceptually equivalent to no stimulation. Persons confined in such environments have difficulty sustaining perception, and tend to hallucinate. A-V materials having consistent sensory fields should, obviously, be avoided.

Color Control

A summary of research related to the color of hospital walls suggests that patients seem to recover more quickly if they are placed in blue rooms following major surgery.[6] Blue has also been found to quiet violent inmates in mental hospitals. Yellow is believed capable of producing a sensation of sunlight and warmth. Attractive shades of yellow seem to positively affect the grades of elementary and secondary school students. Some shades of yellow, however, seem to cause nausea. This finding was very disturbing to airline officials a few years ago.

A New York precision-tool plant decided to coordinate the colors of the machinery and the walls. This was done to make the colors as pleasing as possible. These colors, the company reports, reduced absenteeism by 60 percent, reduced rejected parts by 40 percent, and resulted in a 15 percent increase in productivity.[7] Not a bad result for the price of some paint.

Casino operators at Las Vegas use various colors to obtain the attitudes, and thus the performance, they desire. They use a predominance of red, which is considered a warm, exciting color and results in "more action on the floor." They control the casino temperature closely, too, as they feel it also affects the attitudes of the patrons. Even the masters of psychological warfare, the CIA, at their headquarters in Langley, Virginia, colored their doors in yellow, green, purple, blue, and red because "a psychological study concluded the original gray doors were depressing to CIA employees."[8] Look down the corridors of many school buildings and see if you don't share in this feeling of depression.

The standard fluorescent light has an excess of yellow and very little red, violet, or ultraviolet when compared to sunlight, the standard light. It has been argued that even windows or eyeglasses which block specific light frequencies will lead to fatigue, headaches, or other physical and mental problems. Light on mammalian tissue causes chemical reactions within the tissue and neuroendocrine signals to be generated by photoreceptor cells.[9] Ultraviolet light, for example, has been found to be essential for calcium utilization and kidney and cholesterol control. Other wavelengths, or colors, of light have been related to a variety of body functions. Classroom lighting is important because of the relative number of hours students spend indoors as opposed to outdoors in the sunlight (especially during the winter months).

The primary colors used in a classroom should vary depending on the nature of the instructional objectives to be taught in the space. Classrooms, offices, study carrels, or media centers where active responses are desired will be enhanced if reds are used, as opposed to dark blues or greens. If passive participation is desired, then these objectives may be facilitated by using blues or greens. Blues or greens would also seem desirable for recreation and therapy spaces. Pale colors will make a room look larger. Use cool colors (blue, green, yellow-green, and violet) in south facing, warm rooms. Use warm colors (yellow, orange, red) in north facing, cold rooms.

Long corridors can be visually shortened and turned into interesting patterns by painting the doors and the spaces above them in a bright though darker tone, with the wall spaces in between painted a lighter contrasting tone. Stairwells and walls at the ends of the corridors can be painted with lighter, brighter accent colors to create a visually shorter corridor.[10]

In summary, it appears that the color of the learning environment can consistently affect behavior. It appears that educators and architects should be quite concerned about what colors the learning spaces are painted.

Key Points

1. Adequate lighting is essential to visual learning tasks. The more detailed the task, the greater the light requirement.
2. The use of instructional technology with CRT displays or projected visual images requires light control. The chalkboard and demonstration areas should be highlighted.
3. Colors are important contributors to learning productivity.

Notes

1. "Some Light Issues." *Progressive Architecture,* September, 1977, pp. 106-11.

2. LaGiusa, Frank, and Perney, Lawrence. "Brightness Patterns Influence Attention Spans." *Lighting Design and Application,* May, 1973, pp. 26-30.

3. LaGiusa, Frank, and Perney, Lawrence. "Further Studies on the Effects of Brightness Variations on Attention Span in a Learning Environment." *Journal of the Illuminating Engineering Society,* April, 1974, pp. 249-52.

4. "Study Shows Fluorescent Lights Cause Hyperactivity in Children." *Phi Delta Kappan,* February, 1975, p. 441.

5. Logan, H.L. "Bio-Lighting." Presentation at The Lighting Techniques in Architecture Conference, Madison, WI, December, 1969.

6. "How Color Affects Us." *Today's Health,* January, 1969.

7. Ketcham, Howard. "Color Environment and the Learning Process—Number 1." *Spectrum.* Pittsburgh, PA: PPG Industries, n.d.

8. Klurfeld, Jim. "CIA's Unlikely Spies: They Sit and Read." *Los Angeles Times,* December 20, 1978. Part 1B, p. 2.

9. Wurtman, Richard. "The Effects of Light on the Human Body." *Scientific American,* July, 1975, pp. 68-77.

10. "Color and Factory Environment—Number 5." *Spectrum.* Pittsburgh, PA: PPG Industries, 1974.

Chapter Nine

Instructional Media Technology Requirements for Effective and Efficient Learning

Instructional media technology poses new problems to facility designers, since the variety of hardware and software requires space, electrical connections, temperature control, and storage spaces. Traditional educational buildings do not encourage the use of the "new technologies" in education. More productive learning environments are required.

The use of tape recorders, movie projectors, television systems, and record players requires acoustical treatment of the instructional space. The projection of visual images requires room darkening capability. Instructional hardware often consumes more amperage than conventionally wired classrooms permit. Programmed instruction and other forms of media and materials which permit individualized instruction are often more efficient when a classroom space is broken into carrel study areas. The heat generated by electronic equipment, projector motors, projection lamps, television studio lights, and the increased number of partitions (which restrict air flow) must be counteracted by air control systems. If learning space designs are not flexible enough to accommodate these and other instructional media technology requirements, educators will be unable to implement the curriculum as desired. Flexibility of school plant design is essential when designing schools for instructional media.

To be of optimum use, the school plant should be designed according to the curriculum and the materials which will probably be used. Function should determine the shape of the building; the building should not limit the kinds of media and, thus, the curriculum. To permit construction of this kind, the architect must have information about:

(1) the educational activities and the objectives of the various departments to be housed in the school, and

(2) the manner in which the teachers hope to work with their students.

Learning spaces for the individual must be incorporated into the school environment, if individualized instruction techniques are to be used. Large-group instruction techniques (using film or television) require spaces where the large number of viewers can gather and learn. The trick to tailoring the school plant to accommodate instructional media and other emerging or changing needs is to eliminate load-bearing walls and other interior space limiting designs so that the building can be modified in the future.

Since acoustical and visual control problems were discussed in earlier chapters, only specific problems related to the use of instructional media are included in this chapter.

Audio Media

Media systems which record and/or amplify sound include: tape recorders, phonograph players, sound-motion picture systems, learning (language, electronic) laboratories, dial-access systems, telephone-based systems, and television (including videotape). Lest we forget, the human voice also produces sound.

Tape recorders, phonograph players, television equipment, and motion picture projectors normally require only electrical power, the appropriate materials, and occasionally the ability to darken a room. Dial-access systems, telephone-based audio systems, computer-based systems, and closed-circuit television systems require cabling to conduct the desired "signal" to the student. Conduits for immediate or future cabling should always be built into a new or remodeled educational facility.

The audio produced by motion picture projectors, television, tape recorders, and phonographs is amplified and "broadcast" through a speaker so it can be heard by one or more users. As this is done, some attention must be given to ways of keeping the sound within limits. The sound should not bother students involved in other activities. Architects may do this by soundproofing some instructional areas, or by providing terminal boxes into which the individual students may plug headsets.

Some audio systems, such as dial-access and language laboratory systems, have headsets for individual student use and do not have the above mentioned sound transmission problem. These systems, however, do have cabling problems. When dial-access, language laboratory, or television distribution systems are designed into a building, spaces for material storage, recording, duplication, playback, and use must be considered.

Public address systems should be considered by designers as they develop building specifications. A "P.A." system and/or telephone system for student announcements, current events broadcasts, security, and for administrative purposes may be desired.

Visual Media

As suggested earlier, for effective viewing of projected visual stimuli, it is frequently desirable to reduce the overhead lighting. To plunge the classroom suddenly into total darkness restricts the students' ability to take notes and promotes undesirable, unsupervised behaviors, such as talking, carving on the desks, sleeping, and other non-task related activities. Provision for dimming the overhead lights is most desirable. An option to dimming is to have supplemental lighting systems for controlled brightness, such as a series of adjustable-aim spotlights focused on the students' desks.

If a projector is used to show materials on a *front projection screen,* the light level in the room should be greatly reduced. The overhead projector requires the least light reduction (often none), and the opaque projector requires the most. The amount of light at the source, and the efficiency of the optical system, affect the amount of light projected onto the screen, and thus the amount of light reduction necessary in the room.

The Society of Motion Picture and Television Engineers recommends the following ambient light levels for front projection media:

1. Television projection—five to ten foot-candles.
2. 16mm motion picture projection with normal lumen output—five to ten foot-candles.
3. 16mm motion picture projection with high lumen output—15 to 25 foot-candles.
4. 35mm motion picture projection with normal lumen output—15 to 25 foot-candles.

There are four types of projection screens. A concave aluminum screen, with its efficiency in reflecting light, permits a higher light level in the viewing area. A "matte surface" is a non-glossy screen which has a wide viewing angle. The "beaded surface" has small glass beads on the surface which give a high reflectance or brightness level within a narrow viewing angle. The "lenticular finish" has a serrated plastic surface giving a relatively high brightness level over a relatively wide area. In general, a "matte finish" is used when there is a large audience over a wide area and plenty of light from the projector. A beaded screen, or an aluminum screen, is used when there is a long, narrow viewing area and/or a projector with low light output.

Figure 9.1 suggests the correct relative position for various projectors.

A *rear projection* screen presentation system (see Figure 9.2), usually requires less light reduction but more projection space than front projector systems—often an expensive trade-off. Rear projection systems using mirrors to "bend" the image may reduce

Figure 9.1

Projector Locations

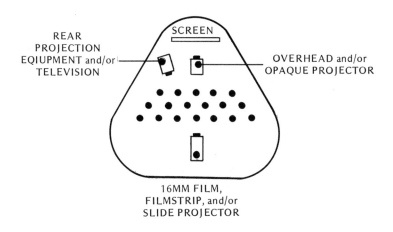

REAR
PROJECTION
EQIUPMENT and/or
TELEVISION

SCREEN

OVERHEAD and/or
OPAQUE PROJECTOR

16MM FILM,
FILMSTRIP, and/or
SLIDE PROJECTOR

Figure 9.2

Front and Rear Projection Screen Locations

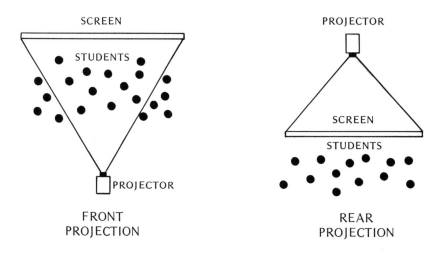

SCREEN

STUDENTS

PROJECTOR

FRONT
PROJECTION

PROJECTOR

SCREEN

STUDENTS

REAR
PROJECTION

the space required for projection, but large rear projection screens usable with a group of 30 or more students are difficult to design without consuming much valuable space.

Determining the appropriate *size of a projection screen* is fairly straightforward. The room size determines the size of the screen. The width of the screen should be approximately one-sixth the distance from the front of the room to the last row of students. The first row of students should be back twice the width of the screen.

Usually, 16mm motion picture projectors, slide projectors, and filmstrip projectors are placed in the center-back of the room. To fill the screen with the projected image, the focal length of the lens in the projector must be chosen with care.

A viewing angle exceeding a line 30° from the perpendicular surface of the projection screen is undesirable. The distortion of the image and the brightness of the image make learning from the projected image difficult. These guidelines for selecting the correct screen size and focal length lens are for matte screens, the most used screen surface today. Glass beaded screens have a narrower viewing angle and more depth capacity.

In order to prevent "keystoning" of the projected image on the screen, where one side of the image (often the top) is larger than another side of the image, a line from the projector to the screen surface must be made perpendicular. Frequently, an overhead projector will be located on a desk top lower than the center of the screen, and the image at the top of the screen will be larger than at the bottom. This may be corrected by pulling the bottom of the screen back toward the front wall so that the distance from the projection lens to the top and to the bottom of the screen is approximately the same.

Avoid illumination levels above 70 foot-candles where rear projection equipment is going to be used. Higher light levels will "wash out" the image on a television screen, microfilm projector, computer CRT display, or other rear screen presentation.

Still visual images may be projected by filmstrips, 2 x 2 slides, or an overhead projector. *Filmstrips* have a fixed sequence which is an advantage in that the order cannot be inadvertently rearranged by a student with coordination problems, but it is a disadvantage in that a teacher cannot reorder the slides or replace a visual as necessary in the filmstrip sequence. Filmstrip projectors are relatively simple to operate and are inexpensive.

Slide projectors usually use trays to keep the individual slides in order. The slides are relatively easy to make with accessible camera equipment. Filmstrips are produced with another type of camera. As the slides are in individual mounts, they may be easily ordered or reordered. Unfortunately, many a presentation has gone awry when the slides fell out of the tray into a pretty pile. A remote control with a 20-foot cord (650 cm) (or more) will permit a teacher to move away from the projector for whatever purpose. A zoom lens on a slide or filmstrip projector will allow the teacher to place the projector in a convenient location and still fill the screen.

An *overhead projector* (see Figure 9.3) is usually situated in front of the audience. It projects transparencies which may have been previously prepared, or the teacher may write on acetate, as he or she would on the chalkboard. The lights may be left on when an overhead projector is used.

In addition to the above mentioned projected sources of still images, there are several other ways to make still visuals available to the student. An opaque projector which reflects light from a printed page or sheet may be used, but it requires room darkening. Microfiche and other microform systems are being increasingly used in instruction, but as yet, there is no standard size, format, or hardware system. Still images may also be presented on a chalkboard, on a posterboard, a handout, or in a text. These media are well-known and require no unusual facility designs.

Moving images may be presented to students by either motion pictures or by television. The 16mm motion picture projection system has been adopted in the western world for instructional purposes. 8mm is used for individuals, but it should be considered by emerging nations as the primary classroom medium for motion

Figure 9.3

Overhead Projector Used for
Small-Group Instruction

Photo Credit: Rogers/Nagel/Langhart Architects. Prospect Valley Elementary School, Denver, Colorado.

pictures. The quality of the projectors and the resolution available in the film make 8mm systems desirable, especially as the space required for the film is greatly reduced. The weight and cost of the projectors are also somewhat less than that of 16mm projectors.

When designing classrooms for these projectors, place circuits in the rear of the classroom for the motion picture projector, for the slide projector, and for the filmstrip projector. Another outlet at the front of the classroom is needed for the overhead projector, tape recorder, and any rear projection equipment which may be used by the teacher. Receptacles along the walls for use of the students who want to individually view materials are also required.

Film and tape storage areas should be maintained within temperature and humidity limits. Film should be stored in an area with a relative humidity between 25 and 60 percent at temperatures below 80°F (27°C). Audiotape should be stored in an area with a relative humidity between 20 and 80 percent at temperatures between 60° and 90°F (15° and 32°C). The films and/or tapes will deteriorate much more rapidly, if they are not kept within these limitations.

The rapid development of relatively low cost "portable" videotape recorders, receivers, special effects generators, and black-and-white cameras make television possible for almost every school (as well as home). The cost of color cameras is still prohibitive for many, but the rest of the color system should be color compatible, so that when the cost of color cameras comes down, the existing equipment will be ready to serve the school needs.

The allocation of the 2500-2690 MHZ frequency range by the FCC and the requirement in many areas that cable TV systems make television distribution capability available to the schools have reduced the problems in using instructional television (ITV). In many schools, there is little demand or available "content" to put into the ITV system. The hardware is relatively inexpensive and reliable—the problem of using ITV seems to relate to a feeling that the existing materials can be better presented in other ways.

It may also be that many educators in the United States are simply not ready—by training or attitude—to accept ITV. Many developing countries in the Middle East and South America are investigating and adopting ITV systems. A few countries are even having engineers examine the feasibility of using satellite distribution of the television programs.

There are basically four ways of transmitting and distributing television programs:

(1) open circuit broadcast systems using the conventional VHF and UHF frequencies received by most "home receivers";

(2) over-the-air closed-circuit systems using microwave transmission and 2500 MHZ ITFS;

(3) coaxial cable distribution systems; and

(4) videotape, videocassette, and videodisc systems.

Open circuit broadcast systems are well-known to most television viewers, as they involve the use of the frequencies and transmitters and receivers used for home viewing. The major advantage of this distribution system is that the public can view the programs which permit credit programs, for example, to be developed for home use.

The over-the-air closed-circuit systems using infrared, microwave, or 2500 MHZ ITFS transmission restrict the viewers to those having the special equipment necessary for reception. Microwave is a loose term identifying a spectrum of frequencies above 890 MHZ. These frequencies are transmitted from point to point, and the receiving antenna must be in line of sight of the transmitter. This type of transmission is often used for connecting a studio with a transmitter at a separate location or a user school site.

The 2500 MHZ system was authorized by the FCC in 1963 for educational users. The frequency range is from 2500 to 2690 MHZ (2690 megacycles). This system is sometimes called the Instructional Television Fixed Service (ITFS) system. This system easily permits sufficient frequencies for audio "feedback" from the receiving location back to the transmitting location, which is often desirable. Relatively few of the allocated frequencies have been requested and used by educators.

Coaxial cable systems provide direct connections within a building, or they may provide cable connections within an entire community. Reception is more reliable when signals are sent via cable, since the cable is not subject to atmospheric or geographic (hills and other terrain features which block the broadcast signals) interference. You can send television-like pictures via "slow scan" techniques by using regular voice grade telephone wire, but to obtain the frequency range needed for conventional television, a coaxial cable must be laid between the transmitting and receiving locations.

It is probable that in the near future a majority of schools in the United States will possess videotape, videocassette, or videodisc systems, providing for the handy and flexible showing of television presentations without the use of a central distribution source for the TV signal. Videotape and videocassette units also permit the teacher to do his or her own programming, often with the assistance of students. Even very young children have been taught to use videocassette systems, although the reel-to-reel videotape equipment presents some problems, since it is not as easy to use. While the new videodisc systems do not permit local, on-the-spot production, they do have the advantage of low cost for the pre-recorded program material. It is anticipated that a great variety of videodisc programs will become available in the near future for academic purposes, and instructional designers should plan to take advantage of these forthcoming materials.

Satellite distribution of television signals and telephone calls for instruction is fairly common today. The synchronous satellites, which remain stationary over a given point on the earth, provide dependable around-the-clock communication. These satellites have a capacity of over six thousand standard circuits and two full-color television channels. Because of the existing communications channels in the United States and the relative cost of a dedicated satellite for instruction purposes, it is doubtful if many states or school districts will use this distribution system for instruction in the near future. In developing countries, however, which do not have the existing channels of communication, and which have sparsely populated areas or a nomadic population, a satellite communication system for radio, television, or telephone distribution may prove to be desirable.

Television *production equipment,* as mentioned earlier, is fairly inexpensive. A minimum studio might consist of a chain of two television cameras connected to a video switcher in a control room, a microphone connected to an audio control in the control room, a monitor or receiver, and the desired lighting and props. In order to record programs for future use, a videotape recorder is desirable. This minimum studio in black-and-white can be acquired as a package for approximately $5,000. Double the cost and you can purchase a color system. The system can be upgraded by acquiring additional cameras, a film chain to play films through the television system, additional receivers, special effects generators, distribution amplifiers, additional videotape recorders for duplicating tapes, etc.

Developments in the recorder technology and other ITV equipment is so rapid that you will want to visit two or more distributors of television equipment to determine what your needs and purse will warrant. Arrange to have competent technicians install a studio of any size.

If you plan to have a *studio* (see Figure 9.4), here is a guide as to the space requirements. The studio itself should have a minimum of 1,000 square feet. There should be at least 12 feet from the floor to the bottom of the ceiling lights, and at least 14 feet to the ceiling. Maintain a temperature of approximately 70 degrees in the area. The studio should be located away from high ambient noise areas, such as music rooms, shop areas, etc. It should be close to utilities and services. An access door for large pieces of equipment or props should be convenient. The studio should also be close to the preparation or storage areas, and

Figure 9.4

Television Studios Are Dedicated Spaces

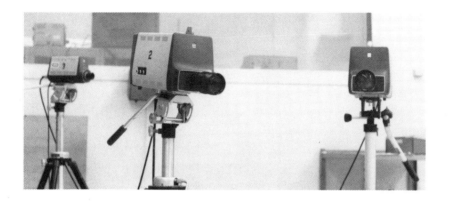

---

adjacent to the control room, and possibly a separate audio recording area. It should be windowless and have specially designed acoustical treatment of the walls and in the air conditioning/ventilation system to prevent fan noises from being picked up in the studio. A window may separate the control room from the studio.

The studio area should have at least six to eight electric circuits. There should be power transformers within 200 feet of video, or audiotape production, or storage areas. Provide electrostatic shielding for power circuits and transformers. Even a small school studio will require air conditioning. Do not use fluorescent lights in the studio. Quartz-iodine or incandescent lamps should be zoned and dimmable. Spotlights should be positioned at about a 45° angle on special ceiling supports. There should be 200 foot-candles of available light in the studio and about 70 foot-candles in the control room.

A standard classroom TV receiver can handle approximately the same number of viewers as the size of the receiver is in inches; i.e., a 25-inch receiver (monitor, television set) can serve approximately 25 student viewers. The receivers may be permanently mounted or on mobile carts. Television reception may also be accomplished through the use of television projectors on either front or rear "projection" screens. With either type of projection system, you must design the screen area so that little or no light falls on the screen.

In addition to these visual materials, there is the "printed page." The textbook, reference work, or programmed instruction book, like the chalkboard, require little attention here beyond a note that glare reduces their effectiveness.

Light control, as discussed in Chapter Eight, is important for the proper use of visual media. Problems involving glare and contrasting light levels are especially critical. Some light in the viewing area is usually desired to decrease eye strain and facilitate the taking of notes.

Distribution Systems

Flexibility in power and communication distribution systems is important. The use of perimeter or under-floor ducts or conduits throughout all buildings will permit the placement of computers, dial-access systems, public address systems, television systems, and electrical power at varying locations. The building should be designed for this flexibility, and the conduits should be included in sufficient size and locations to permit activities in the school to be readily modified either in location or activity. A conduit which carries a television cable could as easily carry a cable connecting computer equipment, etc.

A *dial-access* information distribution system may be compared to the operation of a small telephone company where the students can dial their lessons. The educational specifications compatible with this system include:

(1) individual student control of time and program selection;

(2) immediate access to various pre-recorded materials from a variety of user locations (library, carrel area, home);

(3) freedom of the teacher from content presentations for individual counseling; and

(4) the repetition or review of a lesson by a student.

The problems of adopting such a system involve:

(1) initial capital outlay of funds for the equipment (if teacher-pupil ratios are modified and amortized, cost of using the system may be equal, or less, for a given degree of student learning);

(2) the limited accessibility of software (materials); and

(3) the relatively rapid obsolescence and incompatibility of materials and hardware.

Planning for such a system includes many considerations. What program source will you use (pre-recorded audio and/or video, live audio and/or video)? What technical retrieval system will you use (dial-a-tape via a switching mechanism; dial any desired segment of a taped program; dial an attendant who will put the desired tape on ' for you; have a scheduled time for playback, dial a pre-recorded tape which will record the tape at high speed for the user, thus providing additional user flexibility; or any of the above, connected to the telephone company's equipment so the students can use the tapes anywhere they have a telephone)? What kind of student selection equipment is desired (dial, touchtone, microphone, switch)? What kind of recording or microphone equipment is desired (none, audioactive, record and playback)? Is video playback desired? Is the conduit or cabling available and ready? Will each student have his or her own carrel "office"? What is the desired user/carrel ratio? How many program sources will you want in your system? Where should the student stations and the switching or central area be located? These are a few of the questions to be answered by a designer of a dial-access system.

Another distribution system should be mentioned here. It is neither electronic, nor electric; it is manual. An instructional materials center oriented building may have little need for an electronic distribution system, if it has several copies of its most used materials. The students walk to the materials instead of dialing for them. The cost of the electronic distribution system will usually be significantly higher than the user costs in a "manual" system. In small user situations, less than three or four hundred users per week, the costs are many times more for an electronic distribution system.

Even if a "manual" IMC is planned, conduits should be included in the design of the new facility. Wiring can be pulled through the conduits at little cost, if it is desired at a later time. The conduits provide for flexibility. The cost of putting the conduits into the building as it is being constructed is comparatively very low; extra conduits should be placed into all new school facilities.

A signal from the learning area may be distributed over wires to computer terminals, television receivers, or a student's headset, as appropriate. The signal could also be distributed by an induction distribution system (a local wireless system) instead of by wire. The primary induction coil may be located in or under the carpet or near the ceiling. This induction system would allow students to get either limited electrical power or communication signals anywhere over the carpet through a secondary coil on each chair. Point-to-point lasers or light signals can also distribute communication data to individual students.

Computers in Instruction

Computer technology has been increasing rapidly. In the past ten years, computers have been reduced in size and cost many times. In addition to the uses of computers for payroll, student record keeping, inventory control, and other administrative tasks, computers are employed in education to manage instruction, to assist in the instructional process by providing drill and repetition, and in some cases to provide didactic instruction via modified tutorials.

Distribution of signals from the computer terminals to the central processor is a fairly simple procedure, if conduits have been laid in the buildings where the computers are going to be used. Telephone grade wire systems are acceptable for many computer systems, but some complex visual display systems, like PLATO, require coaxial cable between the components in the system. The power requirements will depend on the specific system which is selected. Many of the new micro-computers being purchased for instructional purposes require little electric power and can be plugged into normal electric outlets.

While computer-managed instruction systems may require only one or two terminals in a classroom area to permit the students to take tests and receive assignments, computer-assisted instruction systems may require a computer terminal for each small group.

A storage area for operating supplies, such as paper, tape, cards, master document files, and similar computer-related materials, should be located adjacent to the main computer room. The storage area should have secure metal cabinets or other fire-proof containers for those documents which would be impossible to replace or are of a confidential nature. In larger systems, space for programming personnel is required.

A wide range of temperature and humidity levels for computer equipment is usually acceptable today.

The extent of anticipated computer operations will determine how much planning must be done to accommodate this technology; one micro-computer can be used virtually anywhere, whereas an extensive CAI system must be planned for in advance.

Key Points

1. Instructional media require room darkening capability, electricity, sound isolation, heat removal capacity, and projection screens. They may require conduits and secure storage areas.
2. The projection screen type and size depend on the depth of the room and its relative width. Rear projection facilities require a substantial amount of room not needed by front projection techniques. The viewing angle from a screen limits the effective width of learning space.
3. There are a variety of ways to distribute television signals.
4. Video, audio, or film distribution may be done by electronic

systems using cable, as in a dial-access system, or manually, as a book would be, in an instructional materials center.

5. The design and construction of a television studio is complex. Lighting, sound control, ventilation, communications between studio and control room, access for large equipment, high ceilings, and humidity control for storage areas are all problems which need special design solutions.

6. Larger computer systems require terminal area(s), a central processing location, conduit and cabling, secure storage, and programming space. New micro-computers, however, can be used in virtually all school rooms.

Chapter Ten

Special-Purpose Facilities
for More Productive Learning

Some teaching-learning activities require special facilities. Due to acoustical needs, specialized equipment, or unique functions, these special facilities include:

(1) libraries and instructional materials centers;
(2) electronic or language laboratories and computer stations;
(3) auditoriums and large-group instructional areas;
(4) music rooms;
(5) physical education areas;
(6) science laboratories;
(7) vocational education shops; and
(8) special education facilities.

The general-purpose classroom will not easily serve the specialized kinds' of activities discussed in this chapter. Most state education departments provide direction in developing the educational specifications for special-purpose facilities. These services should be used to insure that you will be complying with state regulations and requirements.

Libraries and Instructional Materials Centers

The storing of library collections, which tend to double about every 16 years or so, presents a serious space problem to educational administrators. The use of microfiche systems, computerized information storage and retrieval equipment, dial-access carrels, or other forms of technology in the library is not apt to significantly change the size or student capacity of library areas in the near future. The terminals and readers for this equipment consume some space, but more importantly, micro-image materials and programs are not widely available. The use of dial-access or computer terminals in dormitory rooms or student homes for information retrieval purposes may reduce the seating requirements, but this use of these retrieval systems is not gaining popularity rapidly.

As electrical requirements go up (for projectors, tape recorders, better lighting, and information handling devices) and as communication needs increase (for individualized or media-based instructional systems), it is necessary to design and build conduits in library spaces. Perimeter or under-floor ducts must be provided in sufficient numbers and adequate size to permit access to electrical and communications cables at multiple and unpredictable locations as the library grows and evolves.

Air conditioning shafts should also be oversized to provide for possible expansion of the air conditioning system. This is important because of the increasing use of heat-producing micro-image projectors.

To reduce distraction in the library, it is desirable to use sound-absorbing materials. The use of carpeting and the other acoustical treatments discussed in Chapter Seven can be applied to the library.

Instructional materials centers or learning resource centers usually expand the traditional role of a library as a place for books, as follows:

     1. Display and store the books, tapes, films, filmstrips, etc., needed by the teachers or students.

2. Permit individuals to use any materials in carrels which generally restrict undesired visual and audio stimuli.

3. Encourage small groups of students to discuss what they are doing. These centers should be located as close as possible to their users.

4. Permit access to books throughout the reading area.

5. The noise level from moving chairs, mechanical equipment, conversation, and other sources should be kept at a level which does not disturb non-participants.

6. A wide variety of audio and visual stimuli should be easily and instantly accessible.

7. A staff resource and reading area should be isolated from the student area.

8. Checkout and repair facilities for text and nontext materials (and A-V equipment) must be provided.

9. An illumination level of about 70 foot-candles (as suggested in Chapter Eight) and a brightness ratio not exceeding 4 to 1 are desired. Natural light is acceptable if it can be controlled with regard to glare and the brightness ratio.

10. The temperature and humidity should be within the ranges suggested in Chapter Six for the age level and activities expected in the IMC.

Exact space requirements for an IMC will depend upon the expected activities (dial-access information distribution center, computer station, TV production area), the percentage of enrollment expected to use the facility at any one time, and the total enrollment. In determining the activities to be included in the IMC, the answers to the following questions should affect the space requirements:

1. How extensively have the available materials been used in the past?

2. Why would the staff and students change their behaviors?

3. Will funds be available in the near future to equip and staff a new IMC?

4. How innovative has the staff been in the past?

Electronic or Language Laboratories and Computer Stations

An audio facility can be used for many activities calling for a "lecture" or music in various subjects, such as foreign language, dramatics, music appreciation, or even math. Due to the relatively low cost of this information storage and retrieval tool (as compared with staff salaries), it is the basis of several instructional systems. Tapes or audio cassettes, instead of records or discs, are usually used due to ease of operation. In addition to specialized furniture and audio equipment, designers must be sure to provide ample electrical power lines and outlets during construction. Where the decision has been made to install separate computer rooms or stations, especially the larger-scale systems, adequate provisions must be made for electrical service, cooling, lighting, and acoustics.

Auditoriums and Large-Group Instructional Areas

An auditorium is required in many schools to provide an area for:

(1) large-group teaching or presentation and display activities; and

(2) performances and programs of a public nature developed by the students or others in the community.

Instructional television, films, or lectures may be given in an auditorium, as they require little interaction and can be presented to a large number of students at one time. Because of the large numbers of "viewers," audio amplification is often required and, thus, acoustical isolation must be considered. The large number of individuals creates a great deal of heat, which must be taken from the auditorium by air conditioning or other means.

As large-group instructional areas are used infrequently in many schools, planners often design divisible auditoriums so that the large area can be reduced to smaller sections, which can be used as classrooms, band practice rooms, etc.

Another way of increasing the use of an auditorium is to design the area as a combination *cafeteria-auditorium.* This specification will almost certainly call for movable seats and a level instead of a banked floor, but these trade-offs usually increase the use of the large spaces.

Yet another way of using large-group spaces, when the instructional program doesn't often call for large groups of students, is by designing a gymnasium-auditorium. Like any combination room, this area is neither an ideal gym nor auditorium. The proscenium arch of the stage is usually located on the side of the gym, and thus, desirable viewing areas are low in relation to the size of the seating area—the viewing angle is extremely wide. Security of stage equipment and the use of the stage (for rehearsals, etc.) and gym at one time is difficult, unless a movable wall is available to isolate the areas.

An auditorium should be located on the main floor to expedite community access to the building. A lobby, toilet facilities, drinking fountains, public telephones, ticket booth, dressing rooms, and storage facilities must be considered for location adjacent to the auditorium.

Music Rooms

The specifications for music rooms should reflect school and community interests, other available facilities in the community, the school's trend in music offerings, projected needs, and other possible uses for music rooms. Conventional classrooms can usually be used to teach theory and appreciation classes, but rehearsal and/or practice rooms for choral and instrument may also be needed, along with storage rooms for instruments, uniforms, or robes, and a music library. The music offices may include a small repair shop.

The acoustical considerations discussed in Chapter Seven apply to these areas. The control of reverberation, loudness (deadening or separation and/or amplification), and background noise control should be of special concern in the design of the music rooms.

Physical Education Areas

Access to the outside for community service should be considered for the physical education areas. As with the auditorium, the gym should be usable by the community without compromising the security of the remainder of the building.

Boys' and girls' locker areas should have toilets nearby. The shower, drying, and dressing areas should have approximately 20 foot-candles of light; air temperature in the high seventies; and should be well ventilated. Other factors to consider when planning physical education facilities include:

1. Acoustical treatment is needed to reduce noise and echo.
2. The design and materials selected should be able to minimize maintenance.
3. The facilities should be isolated from classroom areas where the noise would be distracting.
4. Non-slip floors and non-abrasive and rounded corners should be required for safety purposes.
5. Windows, if any, in gymnasiums should be elevated and protected. Ventilation is important in the physical education area, and the windows may be included in the ventilation plan.
6. First aid facilities should be accessible.
7. The main entrances/exits should swing out and be convenient to the traffic pattern in the rest of the school.
8. Spectator areas, if provided, should have accessibility to toilets, parking, and the rest of the building.
9. The selection of flooring surfaces is quite varied and will require the special attention of the architect.

A direct entrance to the locker rooms from the outside playground will reduce the amount of dirt, and thus wear, to corridor and classroom areas. Toilet facilities and drinking fountains should be available to students using outdoor physical education facilities. The storage of nets, balls, bats, etc., should be as convenient as possible.

Science Laboratories

The specialized materials and equipment needed for biology, chemistry, and physics usually require separate laboratory facilities for each of these subjects. Combining the classroom and laboratory area may reduce the total space requirement and may allow the science program to be more flexible. Individuals or groups may work in these combined areas on projects, or may receive instruction at one time under the overall guidance of one instructor.

Chemistry laboratories, especially, need an efficient air exhaust system. Physics areas need multiple variable A-C and D-C electrical current facilities. Water and sinks are necessary in all laboratories. Air and gas outlets are needed in most laboratories. All laboratories need secure storage areas for materials, chemicals, and equipment. Movable, specialized chairs and tables are required.

The lighting in these areas should be uniform at about 100 foot-candles with few shadows. The flooring in the physics and biology areas may be vinyl, or asphalt tile, or carpeted. The chemistry floor should be selected to resist the corrosive action of chemicals.

Vocational Education Shops

Schools are increasingly considered service agencies to the entire community, so more emphasis is being placed on industrial and vocational programs. The industrial art areas should be planned to provide flexibility with regard to space and equipment. This flexibility is needed to permit a wide range of projects and activities. Shop areas may be needed for work with metal, wood, plastics, electricity, etc. Drafting areas are also often required.

The space needs for vocational programs include: areas for conventional instruction, small-group instruction, individual counseling, reference materials, storage, exhibition, and project assembly. Safety and fire control considerations should be constantly examined when these areas are designed. Access to a service entrance for the delivery of materials and equipment is desirable.

Storage areas are always needed. All machines should be equipped with convenient start/stop breaker switches, and other emergency switches should be located throughout the shops. Potentially dangerous lathes, band saws, and other equipment should have 100 foot-candles of light and safety guards whenever possible. Acoustical treatment of the shop area is essential. The wall surfaces should be of materials that are easily cleaned. In addition to a high electrical capacity, the shop areas should have plumbing for hot and cold water. The students should have places where the projects they are working on can be stored between classes.

Special Education Facilities

Special education facilities are usually provided for students who are mentally, physically, and/or emotionally handicapped. According to the definitions accepted by various state departments of education, from ten percent to 15 percent of the total pupil population falls into the special education category. It includes the blind, or near blind, crippled, hearing impaired and deaf, mentally retarded, and the emotionally disabled.

Usually, these areas are designed for a limited number of students. The maximum enrollment in most states is eight to 11 pupils in kindergarten through junior high school, and ten to 12 in high school. The "mainstreaming" trend, mandated by legislation at the national level in the United States, is resulting in many of these pupils being placed into regular classrooms. If mainstreaming continues to work successfully, there will be fewer facilities needed for the handicapped in the future, although it is anticipated that not *all* handicapped children will be able to function effectively in regular classrooms, and thus some special education facilities will continue to be needed. In order to encourage the greatest feasible degree of mainstreaming, all special education rooms should be located close to the regular classrooms.

Special education classrooms should have:

(1) adjacent toilets;

(2) areas for isolation and rest;

(3) a parent conference area;

(4) auditory testing and training area;

(5) perception testing and training area; and

(6) a psychological testing area.

Buildings to house special education students should include:

(1) ramps instead of steps and curbs (one to 12 maximum gradient);

(2) wide doors and corridors (32 to 36 inches, or 80 to 90 cm);

(3) wide toilet entrances (48 inches or 120 cm minimum) (with grab-bars);

(4) low elevator buttons;

(5) low telephones;

(6) at least one major building entrance should have an automatic door with a time-delayed closing;

(7) safety glass in doors and low windows;

(8) no sharp corners and surfaces;

(9) hardware on doors, drinking fountains, etc., that can be used by the blind and physically handicapped;

(10) "tardy bells" and fire alarms with both visual and audio components so both the blind and deaf can be alerted; and

(11) special attention to colors, to either stimulate or tone down activities, depending on the children involved.

Key Points

1. The majority of teaching spaces are general areas where all subjects can be taught, but there are some dedicated teaching spaces for specific activities. These areas include: special education facilities, music rooms, shop rooms, science laboratories, language laboratories, instructional materials centers, auditoriums, and physical education areas.

2. Instructional materials centers serve a wider range of objectives than do libraries. They require special lighting consideration when microform readers or computer terminals are used. They

should have small-group study tables and individual study areas. The use of specialized readers, projectors, and recorders demands a large electrical load capability and a heat elimination system.

3. Special education areas require the special design of all facilities.

Chapter Eleven

Equipping the Learning Environment

The development of specifications related to the equipment and furnishings needed in a school building should be part of the original overall educational specifications. The furniture should be usable in different locations and for different purposes. It should be adaptable enough to meet all anticipated learner requirements. Left-handed students and/or students with varying size body frames or postures need furniture and playground equipment which fit them. The implementation of modern educational philosophies requires more flexible room arrangements, and it is necessary that furniture and equipment today be movable.

In ordering equipment or furnishings for a school, the following considerations should be included:

1. The appearance should harmonize in color and style with the rest of the furnishings in the immediate instructional area. See Figure 11.1.
2. The availability of the equipment should be determined so that delivery dates are realistic and acceptable.
3. The building codes must be determined prior to purchasing new equipment. Many states have lists of tested and acceptable items.

Figure 11.1

Modern Furniture

Photo Credit: Rogers/Nagel/Langhart Architects. Prospect Valley Elementary School, Denver, Colorado.

---

4. The comfort of a piece of equipment should be determined so that the "child-furniture" interface is appropriate. In addition to the size of the equipment, light reflection, color, and the acoustics of the items should be considered.
5. The flexibility of the item to fulfill varying requirements of the school should be considered. Is it adjustable? Movable? Does it have multiple uses?
6. The guarantees should be identified and compared when initial costs are considered. The reputation of the seller should also be weighed.
7. The cost, durability, and maintenance requirements of the item should be determined. It is desirable, of course, to have furnishings and equipment which need little or no maintenance. Ask the manufacturer to provide samples. Test them. Replacement parts should be easily obtained and installed. Be concerned with life cycle costs rather than simply initial costs. Life cycle costs include the initial cost, the cost of money spent (interest), installation costs, operation costs, and maintenance.
8. The safety of the item should overshadow all other considerations. If it appears that the item will easily tip over, pinch, collapse, scratch, shock, or otherwise harm students or staff, it should be rejected. All materials and furnishings should be non-combustible, non-toxic, and non-allergenic. All edges should be rounded.

The above considerations must be weighed against each other and a selection made on the basis of the best available data. Economic considerations should be overshadowed by safety considerations.

The educational specifications may prescribe areas for student isolation and solitude. This may be accomplished by carrels in the library or the corridors. Where possible, this can be done outside of the building by providing one- or two-person benches in areas not near footpaths.

The positioning of chairs too closely together may produce undesired anxiety in some students. Crowding may intrude upon an individual student's personal space to the degree he or she feels uncomfortable. Additionally, straight rows tend to confine the students' attention to the teacher—which is fine only if administrative control is desired more than student interaction.

Studies indicate that leaders tend to sit at the *head* of a table. It appears that leaders tend to take this position, but it also appears that the position, if assigned or selected, may affect or encourage leadership characteristics.[1] If the development of leadership is one of the instructional goals, it may be desirable to have situations where all of the students must on occasion occupy such "head" positions.

Other studies indicate that students are quite verbal depending upon where they sit.[2,3,4] In conference situations, the students sitting on the side of a table will be significantly quieter than those sitting opposite the instructor. In classroom situations, the students in the first row will participate more than other students. The students in the middle will participate more than those in the end rows. Movement of student seats on a regular basis may be desirable, if overall participation is desired. Occasionally, moving the chairs into a circle may also desirably affect student participation patterns.

Writing Specifications and Purchasing

Once the determination has been made to purchase a specific type of equipment, the quantity and quality of the furnishings or equipment must be described. Specifications should indicate where the item is to be delivered or placed. They should also specify if the item is to be assembled by the manufacturer.

The specifications may be written by the architect or by the purchasing agent for the school district. If the architect develops the specifications, he or she will normally add overhead and profit percentage to the total cost of the bill for this service. Many school districts will have the architect arrange the purchasing and installation of the fixed items. The school may purchase the movable items, including furniture. The degree to which the architect is paid a fee to supervise the ordering and installation of equipment and furnishings is a decision the school board must make.

It is often desirable to request both unit bids and total package bids for groupings of equipment, as in a science laboratory. This often invites increased price competition among the bidders for the total contract. It also allows the school district to award the separate contracts to the low bidders for each type of equipment.

Specifications should be written by a team of people so that individuals knowledgeable about writing specifications can work with persons who understand the functions to be performed in the building. The purchasing and installation specifications mentioned here apply to the instructional technology equipment needed in the building.

It is desirable to be aware of specific bidding problems. In some localities, you will be able to mention brand names in the specifications. Care should be taken to include all relevant information, as an omission may mean that you will obtain bids for unsatisfactory products. Common sense is a vital ingredient in developing furniture and equipment specifications.

The procedure for soliciting bids for equipment and furniture is that once the specifications have been developed, it is desirable to advertise the bidding so that as many suppliers and manufacturers as possible will compete for the order. The specifications, or bidding documents, often including drawings, should be given to the suppliers at least two weeks before bids are expected.

The opening of the bids should occur at a previously specified time and place. The evaluation of these bids should include a hard look at the item specifications. Note the bid security and delivery dates. Where furnishings are involved, it may be desirable to have the bidders submit or present samples and catalogs along with their bids. The contract should be awarded to the lowest bidder who meets or exceeds the specifications. Be sure the specifications, however, include installation, repair, and similar competence requirements, or the lowest bid may not wind up being a "best buy." Constant attention to the development of the specifications, the bidding process, and the purchasing of a piece of equipment or furnishings is important.

If installation is a part of the contract, it is important that the completion date and the installation location be specified. As electrical or plumbing connections must be made to some items, it is often desirable to have the architect do the specifications and supervise installation. The problems encountered in carpeting a school may also make it worth the expense to have the architect contract for, and supervise, the installation of this item.

Furniture

Ideally, furniture should be comfortable, visually stimulating, safe, and flexible enough to be used whenever necessary. Chairs or seating must be durable enough to take the uncorked energy expended by vigorous youngsters and their sharp pencil points. They should be light enough to be moved (and perhaps stacked) by the students. The chairs should fit the children. This will often mean that many classrooms will have varying sized furniture. Since few children, of any age, are capable of yoga-like immobility, the furniture also needs to be designed for some movement. See Figure 11.2.

Consider wheels and swivels, as they permit some shifting about—especially for high school students and adults. If arm rests are to be attached to the chair, they should permit the arms to rest at a 90° angle to the body. Don't forget the left-handed students. Fabric covering, as opposed to vinyl, is relatively expensive and it will have a shorter life, but it "breathes" and is more comfortable. Adults will especially appreciate fabric covering.

Hinged top desks are seldom used any more as fingers are caught in them so easily. Moving parts are the first "links" to break. Plastics or other man-made materials are frequently used for writing surfaces because of the hardness and scratch resistance

Figure 11.2

A *"Teaching Hill"*

Photo credit: Perkins & Will. "Teaching Hill" at the Tri-Valley Elementary School, Grahamsville, N.Y.

of such surfaces. These surfaces should reflect relatively little light.

Blackboards are giving way to the green (and other colored) chalkboards which tend to be easier on a student's eyes—they reduce glare and contrast. These boards may have a metal backing so they can be used with magnets to hold signs, letters, etc.

Play Equipment

Playground equipment, necessary for the various age levels of children, should be safe and rugged. All joints and moving parts should have safety guards to prevent pinching and shearing action. The areas under climbing equipment should be sandy or have other soft material under them. In general, swings, slides, and teeter-totters hold up well on elementary school playgrounds and allow the children to develop their gross-motor skills. Some insurance companies feel these items are dangerous, however, and may charge a higher premium if you use them. Volleyball equipment, baseball equipment, and similar materials are available through many reputable suppliers. The criteria discussed in the beginning of this chapter should be applied in the selection of the larger and more expensive equipment.

The availability and placement of equipment and materials are among the most effective predictors of program quality. When the quality of the outdoor recreation areas decreases, the degree of teacher restriction and control increases, and the teacher's attitude appears less friendly, while the children seem to lose interest, and conflict rises.

When designing playground equipment, consider the community's need for a recreation area. The enclosing and restricting of baseball, football, track, and kite-flying spaces in the evenings and on weekends may not be desirable.

Equipment designed for classroom use should be sturdy, have no sharp edges, have few moving parts, be attractive, and consume no more space than necessary. It is desirable that the equipment not entail a great deal of time to either set up or clean after its use. A listing of carrel, furniture, and media suppliers is found in Appendix G.

Key Points

1. Furniture and furnishings for instructional areas should be, first of all, *safe*. They should have rounded corners and no moving parts which can pinch. They should be non-combustible, non-toxic, and non-allergenic.
2. A low first cost becomes an economical choice only if the "life cycle" cost is also low.
3. When writing specifications for the competitive bidding of furnishings, be specific in detailing what you want and will accept.

Notes

1. Sommer, Robert. *Personal Space: The Behavioral Basis of Design.* Englewood Cliffs, N.J.: Prentice-Hall, Inc., 1969, pp. 20-25.

2. Sommer, Robert. "Classroom Ecology." *Journal of Applied Behavioral Science,* 1967, pp. 489-503.

3. Delefes, P., and Jackson, B. "Teacher-Pupil Interaction as a Function of Location in the Classroom." *Psychology in the Schools,* 1972, pp. 119-23.

4. Wulf, Kathleen M. "Relationship of Assigned Classroom Seating Area to Achievement Variables." *Educational Research Quarterly,* Summer, 1977, pp. 56-62.

Appendix A

Evaluation of Existing
School Facilities

Name of School .... Occupancy Date ....

Name of Architectural Firm ....

Name of Contracting Firm ....

1. Site and Grounds
    a.   ...... General development and beautification of site.
    b.   ...... Proximity to students' homes.
    c.   ...... Accessibility by roads, sidewalks, and public transportation.
    d.   ...... Adequacy of facilities for play.
    e.   ...... Free from traffic, electrical, and other dangers.
    f.   ...... Free from noise, smoke, and dust.
    g.   ...... Appropriate drainage.
    h.   ...... Adequate water and sewage disposal.
    i.   ...... Adequate parking facilities for faculty, staff, students, and visitors.
    j.   ...... Adequate bus loading, student walkways, and vehicle traffic patterns.

2. Classrooms and Other Educational Spaces in General
    a.   ...... Size (area).
    b.   ...... Function and shape.

c.   ...... Number of areas.
d.   ...... Exit locations, markings.
e.   ...... Storage for pupils.
f.   ...... Storage for teacher.
g.   ...... Equipment.
h.   ...... Furniture.
i.   ...... Safety—non-slip stair treads, fire-resistant materials.
j.   ...... Lockers—student, staff, storage.
k.   ...... Conduits for electronic equipment.
l.   ...... Electrical adequacy.
m.   ...... Special classrooms (home economics, shop, etc.).
n.   ...... Location of projection screens and equipment.
o.   ...... Room darkening capability.

3. Adequacy of Spaces Related to and Supporting Instruction
a.   ...... Library reading room (IMC).
b.   ...... Library workroom.
c.   ...... Individual study spaces.
d.   ...... Seminar rooms.
e.   ...... Resource and special rooms.
f.   ...... Large-group rooms.
g.   ...... Faculty room.
h.   ...... Cafeteria.
i.   ...... Pupil activity rooms.
j.   ...... Materials preparation areas.
k.   ...... Instructional materials storage.
l.   ...... Conference rooms.
m.   ...... Book storage.
n.   ...... General school storage.
o.   ...... Display space.
p.   ...... General office.
q.   ...... Administrative offices.
r.   ...... Duplicating rooms.
s.   ...... Guidance offices.
t.   ...... Health service facility.
u.   ...... Testing room.

4. Arrangement and Location of Facilities in Relation to Total School
a.   ...... Accessibility to administrative offices.
b.   ...... Classroom arrangement and location.
c.   ...... All-purpose room or cafeteria location.
d.   ...... Relation of kitchen to dining area.
e.   ...... Relation of kitchen to service drives.
f.   ...... Location and arrangement of library.

g.   ...... Facilities for physical education.
h.   ...... Location and arrangement of special facilities—art, music, shops, homemaking, etc.
i.   ...... Lockers and pupil storage areas.
j.   ...... Instructional supply and storage facilities.
k.   ...... Pupil traffic flow within the school.
l.   ...... Location of custodial areas.
m.   ...... Adequacy of drinking fountains.
n.   ...... Adequacy of lavatory facilities.
o.   ...... Location of telephones.
p.   ...... Handicapped facilities.

5. Visual Control
a.   ...... Classroom lighting.
b.   ...... Classroom colors.
c.   ...... Lighting in instructional spaces.
d.   ...... Color in instructional spaces.
e.   ...... Lighting in corridors and stairways.
f.   ...... Color in corridors and stairways.
g.   ...... Color considered in selection of furnishings and equipment.
h.   ...... Design and provision for control of glare.
i.   ...... Window design for natural lighting.

6. Thermal Control
a.   ...... Adequacy of ventilation system.
b.   ...... Control of sound generated by ventilation equipment.
c.   ...... Adequacy of heating system.
d.   ...... Control of heating equipment.
e.   ...... Window design for natural ventilation.
f.   ...... Window design for control of heat transmission.

7. Acoustical Control
a.   ...... Sound deadening and reverberation properties in classroom.
b.   ...... Sound deadening and reverberation properties in hallways.
c.   ...... Sound control between teaching-learning areas.

8. Safety and Security Provisions
a.   ...... Design of stairs, composition of treads, and presence of railings.
b.   ...... Absence of dangerous projections inside and outside building.
c.   ...... Adequacy of safety closers on outside doors.
d.   ...... Freedom from slick floors.
e.   ...... Absence of windows which project open at eye level.

f.   ...... Adequacy of emergency lighting.
g.   ...... Security afforded by outdoor lighting.
h.   ...... Location of walks, drives, and play areas relative to safety.
i.   ...... Relative safety of play equipment.
j.   ...... Identification and safeguards of danger areas.
k.   ...... Adequacy of fire protection features and equipment.
l.   ...... Earthquake codes are met.

9. Maintenance and Operation Considerations
a.   ...... Functionality of interior materials.
b.   ...... Functionality of exterior materials.
c.   ...... Adequacy of mechanical equipment.
d.   ...... Adequacy of window and door mechanisms.
e.   ...... Provisions for good drainage of site.
f.   ...... Durability of instructional and play equipment.
g.   ...... Ease of cleaning floors.
h.   ...... Ease of cleaning stairs.
i.   ...... Ease of cleaning heating units.
j.   ...... Ease of cleaning windows and window sills.
k.   ...... Adequacy and location of custodial storage.

10. Workmanship
a.   ...... Masonry
b.   ...... Carpentry
c.   ...... Cabinetry
d.   ...... Painting
e.   ...... Floors
f.   ...... Roof
g.   ...... Heating equipment
h.   ...... Windows and doors

Appendix B

Checklist for Identifying
Facility Requirements

I. ELEMENTARY SCHOOLS

Note: Many of these questions concern architectural specifications (not educational) and thus are not of direct concern to most educators, *but* the architectural possibilities may suggest additional educational specifications.

Is it desirable to have:

	Yes	No
1. a sink in the classrooms or teaching areas for art, science, drinking, and hygienic purposes?		
2. a permanent or movable counter and storage unit(s)?		
3. counter space on both sides of the sink?		
4. multiple electrical outlets in each classroom?		
5. conduits terminating in each classroom?		
6. brightly painted and well-decorated classrooms?		
7. storage facilities for crayons, drawing paper, science materials, play equipment, etc.? (Be sure to check the dimensions of the paper, etc., when determining specs.)		
8. a filing cabinet(s) in each classroom?		
9. movable walls between classrooms?		
10. permanent walls between classrooms?		
11. doors with glass panels at pupil eye level between the classrooms and the corridor?		

Yes | No

12. direct access from the classroom to the out-of-doors?
13. carpeting on the floors in the halls and classrooms?
14. acoustical materials on the edges of the ceilings and on the upper edges of the classrooms?
15. chalkboards for each classroom?
16. bulletin boards for each classroom?
17. projection screens for each classroom?
18. overhead projectors (or other media) built into each classroom?
19. toilets adjoining each classroom for grades K-3?
20. extensive windows in the classrooms?
21. no windows in the classrooms?
22. air conditioned teaching and learning facilities?
23. an Instructional Materials Center near the classrooms or study spaces?
24. independent study carrels?
25. a library "nook" in every classroom?
26. a separate play area and equipment (sandbox, etc.) for Kindergarten students?
27. special education facilities?
28. a gymnasium?
29. an auditorium?
30. a cafeteria?
31. a combination of the above three facilities?
32. an intercommunication telephone and/or public address system?
33. a dial-access information retrieval system?

II. SECONDARY SCHOOLS

Is it desirable to have:

1. individual student wall lockers?
2. movable walls between instructional spaces (classrooms)?
3. doors having a vision strip at the eye level of the pupils between the classrooms and the corridors?
4. a chalkboard (possibly lined appropriately in the music room and the mathematics classroom)?
5. bulletin boards in the classrooms?
6. permanent projection screens in the classrooms?
7. overhead projectors (or other media) built into each classroom?
8. air conditioning?

Yes | No

9. map rails in the social science classrooms?
10. multiple electrical outlets in the classrooms?
11. conduits terminating in all classrooms?
12. intercommunications and/or public address systems to all classrooms?
13. filing cabinets in all classrooms?
14. an office for each teacher (and/or a closet)?
15. extensive use of windows in the teaching and study areas?
16. windowless teaching and studying areas?
17. brightly decorated facilities?
18. individual study carrel areas?
19. one-unit desk and chair combination furniture?
20. carpeting in the halls and classrooms?
21. acoustical materials on the walls and/or ceilings?
22. classrooms clustered by noise level?
23. classrooms clustered by function or projected traffic patterns?

Appendix C

Planning Checklist

I. Teaching-Learning Areas

	Number of Areas		Number of Students	
	Existing	Expected	Existing	Expected
A. Kindergarten	....	....	....	....
B. Elementary Grades	....	....	....	....
C. Intermediate Grades	....	....	....	....
D. High School	....	....	....	....
E. Industrial Arts	....	....	....	....
F. Homemaking	....	....	....	....
G. Music Practice Areas	....	....	....	....
H. Art Rooms	....	....	....	....
I. Science Rooms	....	....	....	....
J. Other	....	....	....	....

II. Library and Instructional Materials Facilities

	Yes	No
A. Reading Room	....	....
B. Work Area for Groups	....	....
C. Individual Study Areas	....	....
D. Office Area	....	....
E. Instructional Technology Production Area	....	....

	Yes	No
F. Inst'l Technology Storage and Distribution	....	....
G. Other	....	....
....	....	....

III. Administrative Facilities

A. Staff Offices	....	....
B. Teachers' Work Area/Offices	....	....
C. Conference Rooms	....	....
D. Storage Areas for Supplies and Equipment	....	....
E. Special Education Areas	....	....
F. Teachers' Lounge Area	....	....
G. Other	....	....
....	....	....

IV. Food Services

A. Central Kitchen	....	....
B. Snack Bar Service	....	....
C. Vending Service	....	....
D. Central Dining Facility (Joint Use Area)	....	....

V. Special Education Services

A. Physically Handicapped	....	....
—Blind or Partially Sighted	....	....
—Deaf or Hard of Hearing	....	....
—Orthopedically Handicapped	....	....
B. Educable Mentally Retarded	....	....
C. Educationally Handicapped	....	....
D. Disadvantaged Other	....	....

VI. Specific Building Space Considerations

A. Interior walls easily movable for flexibility.	....	....
B. Corridors and other circulation areas designed to serve as instructional spaces.	....	....
C. Wall furnishings (chalkboards, etc.) designed for various age groups.	....	....
D. Lighting and air distribution systems permit moving the partitions.	....	....
E. Cabinets and furniture usable as space dividers.	....	....

	Yes	No

F. Exterior glass areas screened from sky brightness, snow glare, etc. ....

G. Designed to reduce heat gain or loss with insulation, reflectance roofing. ....

H. The temperature can be maintained between 68° and 78°F. ....

I. Carpeting used to reduce noise level. ....

VII. What Areas of the Building Will Be Used by the Community?

....
....
....

Appendix D

Summary of Existing Facilities

(See page 148)

Name of School	Factual Data					Qualitative Bldg. Evaluation (Ex, Good, Poor)[1]						Student Capacity	
	Site Area	Date of Const.	Dates of Addns.	Number of Adequate Classrms.[2]	Number of Substandard Classrooms[2]	Site	Bldg. Structure	Lrng. Areas	Custodial Areas	Adm. Area	Over-all Rating	Ideal	Max.
ELEMENTARY													
SECONDARY													

Notes:
1. See Appendix A for a data gathering guide.
2. Record total enrollment and capacity data on separate sheet for art, biology, business, chemistry, science, gym, homemaking, mechanical drawing, music, physics, shop, and other dedicated or special areas.

Appendix E

Summary of Alternative Uses
of Existing Facilities

(See page 150)

Name of School	Current Use Grades and Capacity	Abandon	Continue to Use		Future Effective Uses							
			As-is	Remodel	Grade Levels	Capac-ity	or	Grade Levels	Capac-ity	or	Grade Levels	Capac-ity

Appendix F

Architect Selection Checklist

Item	Firm	Firm .....
1. How have schools who have used the firm liked the services (harmony, estimated vs. final costs)?		
2. What do the architect's services include (borings, landscaping, acoustical control)?		
3. What items are included or excluded in the cost of the work on which the architect's percentage is based?		
4. How quickly has the architect taken on past projects to prepare preliminary plans?		
5. Is the architect to be reimbursed for his or her travel and/or consultants?		
6. Who pays for the services of consulting engineers?		

Item	Firm	Firm .....
7. If separate contracts are let, is extra reimbursement provided the architect for his or her coordination work?		
8. Is additional pay expected for unusual extra work required of the architect?		
9. What is the architect's fee?		
10. What percentage is due upon completion of preliminary plans and estimates?		
11. What percentage is due on completion of final plans and specifications?		
12. How and when are the other payments due to the architect?		
13. What borings or surveys are to be provided, and who pays for them?		
14. What degree of construction supervision does the architect provide?		
15. How does the architect plan to obtain and translate the educational specifications into architectural specifications and plans? Does he or she plan on talking with the educators?		
16. What financial accounting and reporting methods does the architect use?		
17. What cost estimates does the architect furnish?		
18. Who owns the drawings and specifications?		
19. Will alternate plans be presented at the pencil sketch stage?		
20. How many copies of the plans and specifications will the architect provide without additional cost?		

Item	Firm	Firm .....
21. How many final sets of drawings and specifications will be furnished the Board of Education?		
22. How will disputes be settled?		
23. When will the architect start work on this project? When will he or she be able to have completed final working drawings and specifications?		
24. Does the architect's fee include any public relations work beyond brochure sketches?		
25. To what degree does the architect feel he or she should assist in developing ordering specifications for equipment and furnishings? What is his or her fee for such services?		

Appendix G

Carrel, Furniture, and Media Suppliers

I. Study Carrel Suppliers and Manufacturers

Advance Products Co., Inc., P.O. Box 2178, 1101 E. Central, Wichita, Kansas 67214

American Desk Manufacturing Co., Temple, Texas 76501

Audio Tutorial Systems, Div. of Deckmar Design Specialists, P.O. Box 1306, 1440 Canal St., Auburn, California 90016

Califone Int'l Inc., 5922 Bowcroft St., Los Angeles, California 90016

Chris Cross Industries, 83 Clover Ave., Floral Park, New York 11001

Command Products Co., P.O. Box 1577, Evanston, Illinois 60204

Educational Development Laboratories, Inc., Div. of McGraw-Hill Inc., 1221 Avenue of the Americas, New York, New York 10020

Educational Electronics, Inc., 3017 N. Stiles, Oklahoma City, Oklahoma 73105

Educational Technology, Inc., 2224 Hewlett Ave., Merrick, New York 11566

Fleetwood Furniture Co., Electronics Div., P.O. Box 58, 25 E. Washington, Zeeland, Michigan 49464

Gel Systems Inc., 1085 Commonwealth Ave., Boston, Massachusetts 02215

General Carrel Corporation, 70 Richmond Ave., Staten Island, New York 10302

Gladwin Industries, Inc., 2162 Piedmont Rd., N.E., Atlanta, Georgia 30324

Howe Furniture Corp., 155 E. 56th St., New York, New York 10022

Huff and Co., P.O. Box 3675, Stanford, California 98305

Instructional/Communications Technology, Inc., 10 Stepar Pl., Huntington Station, New York 11746

Intelfax, Inc., Exhibitors Bldg., Grand Rapids, Michigan 49502

Learning Resources Manufacturing Co., 716 Federal St., Camden, New Jersey 08103

McNeff Industries, Inc., P.O. Box 10626, 2414 Vinson St., Dallas, Texas 75207

Micro Precision Corp., 55 Ninth St., Brooklyn, New York 11215

Monroe Industries, Inc., 2955 S. Kansas, Wichita, Kansas 67216

MPC Educational Systems, Inc., 35 Fulton St., New Haven, Connecticut 06512

National School Furniture Corp., 2100 Hollywood Blvd., Hollywood, Florida 33020

Radio-Matic of America, Inc., 760 Ramsey Ave., Hillside, New Jersey 07205

Rigid-X Div., Southern School Service, Inc., P.O. Box 867, Canton, North Carolina 28716

Scribe, 3166 DesPlains Ave., DesPlains, Illinois 60118

Synsor Corp., Bldg. 501, 2927 112th St., S.W., Everett, Washington 98204

Worden Co., 1121 Ionia N.W., Grand Rapids, Michigan 49502

II. School Equipment and Furniture Suppliers and Manufacturers

Adirondack Direct, 219 E. 42nd St., New York, New York 10017

American Desk Manufacturing Co., Temple, Texas 76501

American Seating Co., 945 W. Hyde Park Blvd., Inglewood, California 90309

Clarin Manufacturing Co., 4640 W. Harrison St., Chicago, Illinois 60644

Columbia-Hallowell, Standard Pressed Steel Co., Hatfield, Pennsylvania 19440

Educational Electronics, Inc., 3017 N. Stiles, Oklahoma City, Oklahoma 73105

E.F. Hauserman Co., Educators Manufacturing, 3401 Lincoln Ave., Tacoma, Washington 98401

Gym Master Co., 3200 S. Zuni St., Englewood, Colorado 80110

Heywood-Wakefield Co., Gardner, Massachusetts 04345

Highsmith Co., Inc., P.O. Box 25A, Highway 106 E., Ft. Atkinson, Wisconsin 53538

McNeff Industries, Inc., P.O. Box 10626, 2414 Vinson St., Dallas, Texas 75207

Mitchell Manufacturing Co., Milwaukee, Wisconsin 53246

School Days Equipment Co., 951-973 N. Main St., Los Angeles, California 90012

Welch Co., Institutional Furniture, 1615 Santee St., Los Angeles, California 90015

III. Instructional Media Equipment Suppliers

Ampex Corporation, 410 Broadway, Redwood City, California 94063 (Audio and Videotape Equipment)

Audiotronics, 7428 Bellaire Avenue, N. Hollywood, California 91605 (Audio Equipment, Video Cameras)

Bell and Howell, 7100 N. McCormick, Chicago, Illinois 60645 (Audio and Visual Equipment)

Califone International Inc., 5922 Bowcroft St., Los Angeles, California 90016 (Audio Equipment)

Charles Beseler Co., 8 Fernwood Rd., Florham, New Jersey 07932 (Audio and Visual Equipment)

Comprehensive Video Supply Corp., 148 Veterans Drive, Northvale, New Jersey 07647 (Videotape Equipment and Supplies)

Da-Lite Screen Co., Inc., 3100 N. State Road 15, Warsaw, Indiana 46580 (Projection Screens)

Dukane Corp., 2900 Dukane Drive, St. Charles, Illinois 60174 (Audio and Visual Equipment)

Eastman Kodak Co., 343 State St., Rochester, New York 14650 (Cameras, Projectors, and Screens)

Eiki International, Inc., 27882 Camino Capistrano, Laguna Niguel, California 92677 (Projectors)

Fairchild Industrial Products, 75 Mall Drive, Commack, New York 11725 (Audio and Visual Equipment)

GAF Corporation, 140 W. 51st St., New York, New York 10020 (Visual Equipment and Screens)

General Electric Company, Electronics Park 6-205, Syracuse, New York 13201 (Videotape Equipment, Projection Bulbs)

Hamilton Electronics Corp., 2003 W. Fulton St., Chicago, Illinois 60612 (Audio Equipment)

Heathkit Company, Benton Harbor, Michigan 49022 (Electronic Components)

Hoppman Corporation, 5410 Port Royal Rd., Springfield, Virginia 22151 (Projection Equipment, Screens, and Programmers)

Howe Furniture Corp., 155 E. 56th St., New York, New York 10022 (Rear Projection Screens)

JVC Industries, Inc., 58075 Queens Midtown Expressway, Maspeth, New York 11378 (Videotape Equipment)

Kalart Victor Corp., Hultenius Street, Plainville, Connecticut 06062 (Projectors and Videotape Equipment)

Lafeyette Radio Electronics, 111 Jericho Turnpike, Syosset, New York 11791 (Electronic Components)

Newcomb Audio Products Co., 12881 Bradley Ave., Sylmar, California 91342 (Audio Equipment)

Olson Electronics, 260 S. Forge St., Akron, Ohio 44327 (Electronic Components)

Photo and Sound Company, 116 Natoma St., San Francisco, California 94105 (Audio and Visual Equipment Distributor)

Radio Shack, Division of Tandy Corp., 1400 One Tandy Center, Fort Worth, Texas 76102 (Electronic Components, Computers)

RCA Service Company, Cherry Hill Offices, Bldg. 203-3, Camden, New Jersey 08101 (Audio and Visual Equipment)

Sharp Electronics Corp., 10 Keystone Place, Paramus, New Jersey 07652 (Videotape Equipment)

Singer Education Systems, 3750 Monroe Ave., Rochester, New York 14603 (Audio and Visual Equipment and Screens)

Sony Corporation of America, VTR Div., 9 W. 57th St., New York, New York 10019 (Audio and Videotape Equipment)

Spiratone Inc., 135-06 Northern Blvd., Flushing, New York 11354 (Camera Accessories)

3M Company, Visual Products Division, 3M Center, St. Paul, Minnesota 55101 (Overhead Projectors, Microfiche Equipment)

Viewlex, Inc., 1 Broadway Ave., Holbrook, L.I., New York 11741 (Audio and Visual Equipment)

Wollensak/3M Co., 3M Center, St. Paul, Minnesota 55101 (Audio Equipment)

Bibliography

Acoustical Control

Baas, Alan. *Acoustical Environments* (Educational Facilities Review Series). Eugene, Oregon: ERIC Clearinghouse on Educational Management, April, 1973.

Ely, Donald P., Knirk, Frederick G., and Farmer, Charles (Eds.). *Instructional Hardware: A Guide to Requirements.* New York: Educational Facilities Laboratories, Inc., 1970.

Lewis, P.T. "Noise in Primary Schools." *Journal of Architectural Research,* March, 1977, pp. 34-37.

Costs of New Facilities

Isler, Norman. *Cost Factors in the Planning, Designing, Financing, and Construction of Elementary and Secondary Educational Facilities.* Madison, Wisconsin: ERIC Clearinghouse on Educational Facilities, February, 1970.

Meier, James. *Combined Occupancy Development.* New York: Educational Facilities Laboratories, Inc., 1970.

Instructional Technology Requirements

Communications Technologies in Higher Education. Washington, D.C.: Communications Press, Inc., 1977.

Design for ETV: Planning for Schools with Television. New York: Educational Facilities Laboratories, Inc., 1968.

Ely, Donald P., Knirk, Frederick G., and Farmer, Charles (Eds.). *Instructional Hardware: A Guide to Requirements.* New York: Educational Facilities Laboratories, Inc., 1970.

Spangenberg, R., and Smith E. *Handbook for the Design and Implementation of Air Force Learning Center Programs.* AFHRL-TR-75-69, Lowry Air Force Base, Colorado: Air Force Systems Command, December, 1975.

Learning Space Specifications Development

Baas, Alan. *Systems Building Techniques.* Eugene, Oregon: ERIC Clearinghouse on Educational Management, 1972.

Beeken, Don, and Janzen, Henry L. "Behavioral Mapping of Student Activity in Open-Area and Traditional Schools." *American Educational Research Journal,* Fall, 1978, Vol. 15, No. 4, pp. 507-17.

Gwynne, Susan (Ed.). *Guide for Planning Educational Facilities.* Columbus, Ohio: Council of Educational Facilities Planners, 1976.

Knirk, Frederick G. "Learning Space Specifications." *Educational Technology,* June, 1970, pp. 22-25.

Larson, C. Theodore. *The Effect of Windowless Classrooms on Elementary Children.* Ann Arbor, Michigan: University of Michigan, Publication Distribution Service, n.d.

Manufacturers' Compatibility Study. Menlo Park, California: Educational Facilities Laboratories, Inc., 1971.

Light Control

Baas, Alan. *Luminous Environments* (Educational Facilities Review Series). Eugene, Oregon: ERIC Clearinghouse on Educational Management, March, 1973.

Falk, Norman. "New Standards for Classroom Lighting." *American School and University,* March, 1972, pp. 21-28.

LaGiusa, Frank. "Select Lighting with Energy in Mind." *American School and University,* March, 1974, pp. 54-55.

Ott, John. *Health and Light.* New York: Pocket Books, 1976.

Site Planning and Development

Baas, Alan. *Site Development* (Educational Facilities Review Series). Eugene, Oregon: ERIC Clearinghouse on Educational Management, July, 1973.

Gibson, Charles. *School Site Analysis and Development.* Sacramento, California: California State Department of Education, n.d.

VandenHazel, Bessel. "An Ecologist Looks at Modern School Design." *Council of Educational Facilities Planners Journal,* August, 1971, pp. 10-11.

Special-Purpose Facilities

Arts and the Handicapped: An Issue of Access. New York: Educational Facilities Laboratories, Inc., 1973.

Gill, W., and Luke, A. *Facilities Handbook for Career Education.* Washington, D.C.: National Institute of Education, 1976.

Holt, James. "Involving the Users in School Planning." *School Review,* 1974, pp. 707-730.

Johnson, S. *Vocational Education Facilities.* Eugene, Oregon: ERIC Clearinghouse on Educational Management, 1972.

Justin, J. Karl. "Lecture Hall and Learning Space Design." *Journal of SMPTE,* March, 1966, pp. 183-90.

Morgan, Michelle. "Beyond Disability: A Broader Definition of Architectural Barriers." *AIA Journal,* May, 1976, pp. 50-53.

New Jersey State Department of Education. *Educational Specifications.* Trenton, New Jersey: Bureau of Facility Planning, 1973.

Physical Recreation Facilities. New York: Educational Facilities Laboratories, Inc., 1973.

Surveys and Forecasting Techniques

Fredrickson, John. "Effective Planning for Your District." *School Management,* April, 1974, pp. 30 and 33.

Graves, Ben. "Modernization: Everybody's Doing It." *Council of Educational Facilities Planners Journal,* July-August, 1977, pp. 4-7.

Hawkins, Harold. *Appraisal Guide for School Facilities.* Midland, Michigan: Pendell Publishing Co., 1973.

Thermal Environment

Berlowitz, Manfred, Drucker, Eugene, and Scarbrough, William. *Thermal Environment of Educational Facilities.* Albany, New York: State Education Department, Division of Educational Facilities Planning, 1969.

Boyer, Ernest L. "Energy and the Schools." *Today's Education,* September-October, 1977.

The Economy of Energy Conservation in Educational Facilities (Revised). New York: Educational Facilities Laboratories, Inc., 1977.

LeBlanc, Edmond. *Energy Sourcebook for Educational Facilities.* Columbus, Ohio: Council of Educational Facilities Planners, 1977.

Rohles, Frederick. "Thermal Sensations of Sedentary Man in Moderate Temperatures." *Human Factors,* December, 1971, pp. 553-560.

Glossary

Acoustical Control. A process of designing and controlling the sounds in a learning area. In these facilities, the sound level needs to be appropriate to the task(s) to be done by the teacher or student. This process is especially important where audio amplifiers are used in open learning areas.

Air Conditioning. A process of improving the quality or quantity of the air. The air may be dehumidified, humidified, cooled, warmed, or cleaned of dust and pollen.

Brightness. The attribute of visual perception in accordance with which an area appears to emit more or less light.

Brightness Ratio. A term used in discussing the variations of brightness found within the visual environment. Some contrast is desirable in a task area, but high brightness differences in the visual environment are detrimental to visual perception and accuracy and may cause eye strain.

Carrels. Instructional furniture designed to limit the sounds and potentially distracting visual stimuli from disturbing a learner. Carrels usually have partitions raised above a learner's line of sight when he or she is sitting. Many carrels have shelves for books or other materials.

Coaxial Cable. A particular type of cable capable of passing a wide range of frequencies with very low signal loss. Such a cable, in its simplest form, consists of a hollow metallic covering with a single wire accurately placed in the center of the shield and isolated from it.

Computer-Assisted Instruction (CAI). An instructional situation in which a computer analyzes or diagnoses student input, records this input in memory, and then, based on the diagnosis, presents stimulus/instructional materials to the student.

Computer-Managed Instruction (CMI). An instructional situation in which a computer is programmed to analyze or diagnose student input and then record that data in memory. The computer is then programmed to suggest sources of instructional materials the student should go to for instruction. The computer manages the instruction by analyzing the student's knowledge and then suggesting textbooks, slides, tapes, films, etc., for him or her to go to for further instruction.

Contrast. The range of difference between light and dark visual environment; brightness differences within a task area. For each viewing, some contrast in the task area is desirable to attract attention to the task itself.

Educational Specifications. This is data about the educational program which educators obtain to give to an architect to use to develop architectural specifications for a new facility. The specifications usually include the number and type of spaces required, the sizes and special features of the individual spaces, the relationship of the spaces, needed flexibility, etc.

Foot-candle. A unit of illumination on a surface that is one foot from a light source of one candle and equal to one lumen per square foot.

Foot-lambert. Unit of brightness as measured by a photometer. A lumen per square foot is a unit of incident light and a foot-lambert is a unit of emitted or reflected light.

Individualized Instruction. An instructional approach intended to permit different student needs, abilities, and goals to be reflected in a tailored program with goals, and/or pacing, and/or materials, and/or instructional methods differing from other students in the same school.

Instructional Technology. The application of tools and processes to instructional problems which result in predictable "learned" behaviors. The tools and processes may, or may not, involve instructional media.

Joint Occupancy Building. A building which has, in addition to a school facility, either apartments or commercial office spaces. In this type of building, the "school" expands or constricts into the adjacent floors or spaces as the need arises for a larger or smaller "school" area. In some cases, this type of facility can be cost-effective.

Lambert. A measure of luminosity from an emitting or reflecting surface.

Media, Instructional. Devices used in schools to assist in instruction by storing and presenting stimuli to learners. Audio media usually amplify signals on magnetic tape to a level appropriate for student use. Visual media often involve the projection of visual stimuli stored on film or tape.

Multiple-Use Building. See "Joint Occupancy Building."

Open Teaching Space. A classroom without the typical walls separating each teaching station. Often used in team-teaching situations. It is easy to vary the space requirements for groups of varying sizes. Due to potential acoustical problems, it is desirable to carpet or provide other acoustical materials in the facility.

Preliminary Drawings. Drawings and specifications prepared by the architect (from the "educational specifications") in the design state of architectural planning. These drawings must be approved by the necessary local and state agencies. Materials are identified and structural, mechanical, and electrical systems are detailed. Multiple sets of drawings may be prepared so the client can choose between alternative interpretations of the educational specifications.

Remodeling. The process of refurbishing an existing building. The external "facelifting" is relatively unimportant to educators, as it is the internal configuration which limits or facilitates the educational program. Many remodeling programs will eliminate interior walls in order to provide different spaces or to provide greater interior flexibility and an open plan facility to permit future changes.

Survey, Educational Need. The gathering of data needed to make building, remodeling, or abandonment decisions. This survey includes data on the students, school program (current and projected), and existing facilities.

Team-Teaching Facilities. Teaching/learning spaces where two or more teachers work together with a group of students. Because the size of the groups often changes, the open areas must be flexible enough to accommodate groups of varying sizes.

Index

Acoustical control, 24-27, 57, 79-84, 119
Administrative space, 26, 28
Air conditioning, 25, 33, 35, 37, 42, 63, 68-71, 97, 116
Anderson, Robert, 32
Architect, 4, 8, 34, 49, 151
Architectural specification, 9, 23, 33-47
Art rooms, 43
Audio amplifiers, 83, 98
Auditorium, 24, 118

Berlowitz, Manfred, 61, 77
Blair, W.G., 61
Bokelmann, S.O., 77
Brightness, see "Light"
Building codes, 30

Campus plan, 37
Carpeting, 24, 82, 84, 86-88
Carrels, 18-19, 87
Color, 71, 93-94
Computers, 15, 112-113, 118
Conduits, 15, 99
Construction, 43, 47
Consultants, 6

Corridors, 27, 82
Cost estimates, 9, 55-61
Cruickshank, W., 32
Curriculum, see "Educational specifications"

Delefes, P., 133
Detroit Public Schools, 41, 48
Dewey, John, 13, 32
Dial-access, 16, 98-99, 110
Distribution systems, 105-106, 110-112, 117
Downey, Gregg, 77
Drawings, detailed, 34, 59
Drawings, working, 9, 34, 45
Drucker, Eugene, 61, 77

Economics, 3, 9, 55
Educational Facilities Laboratories, 41, 48
Educational specifications, 3, 8, 13, 23, 33-43, 65
Energy, 10, 57, 68, 73-75, 105

Fire, 28
Flexibility, 8, 10, 38, 56, 130
Floor plans, 35-39, 45

Furniture, 29, 125, 125-132, 155
Future needs, 3

Galloway, Charles, 32
Gilliand, John W., 65
Goodlad, John, 19, 32
Greer, George D., 63, 76

Hall, Edward, 17, 32
Handicapped, 30, 122
Harmon, Darell, 77
Heating, 66, 71-73, 97
House plans, 23, 35
Humidity, relative, 65, 69

Individualized instruction, 16, 18,
    23, 87, 97
Instructional design, 13
Instructional media center (IMC),
    18, 21, 25, 43, 112, 116-118
Instructional technology, 23, 93
Insulation, 36, 66-68, 73
Interior design, 24, 26

Jackson, B., 133
Johnson, G., 32
Joint occupancy buildings, 58-59

Ketcham, Howard, 95
Klurfeld, Jim, 95

LaGiusa, Frank, 95
Lane, W.R., 70, 77
Language laboratory, 16, 98
Larson, C.T., 48
Learning, active, 17
Learning, interactive, 16
Learning, nonverbal, 16-17, 128
Learning, passive, 15-16, 22, 43
Library, *see* "Instructional media
    center"
Light, 16, 66, 68, 85-95, 102, 110
Logan, H.L., 95

McCardle, Robert, 70, 77
McVey, G.F., 76
Media, instructional, 8, 83, 86, 90,
    97-113, 117, 131, 157
Meier, James, 61
Mordue, Dale, 77
Multiple-use facilities, 38
Music, 43, 119
Muzak Company, 80

NASA, 64
Needs analysis, *see* "Survey, school
    need"
New York State Education Depart-
    ment, 69
Noise control, 19, 24, 79-84
Nongraded instruction, 19

Offices, 21
Open teaching space, 24, 88
Ott, John, 162

Parking, 30, 50-53
Partitions, 22, 35, 39, 82, 98, 119
Peccolo, Charles, 69
Perney, Lawrence, 95
"Personal territory," 16, 128
Physical education, 29, 43, 120-122
Plans, final, 33, 45
Plans, preliminary, 9, 33
Playground equipment, 29, 51,
    131-133
Prefabricated buildings, 39-40
Program evaluation, 4
Program evaluation review tech-
    nique (PERT), 34
Program planning, 5
Program requirements, *see* "Educa-
    tional specifications"
Programmed instruction, 17, 97
Public relations, 4
Purchasing, 128-130

Remodeling, 5, 9, 11, 135, 147, 149

Safety, 27, 29, 120, 127, 132
Scarbrough, William, 61, 77
School board, 5, 9
School Construction Systems Development project, 41
Schoolhouse Systems Project, 41
Science instruction, 29, 121
Screen, placement of, 100
Self-contained classrooms, 18, 21, 35, 43
Shop areas, 29, 121
Site, school, 4, 9, 30, 33, 49, 53
Social environments, 22
Solar energy, 67, 73-75
Sommer, Robert, 133
Space requirement, 43
Special education facilities, 122-123
Survey, school need, 3, 11, 15, 21, 31, 35, 139, 143, 147, 149
Swimming pool, 29

Systems projects, 40

Team-teaching, 18-21, 23, 37
Television, 15, 86, 97, 99, 105-110, 157
Television studio, 108
Temperature, 41, 63-76, 97

Underground schools, 68-69

Vandalism, 10, 41
Ventilation, 10, 56, 63-74
Visual environment, 24, 41, 87, 91
Visuals, 86-88, 93, 99-110, 131, 157
Vocational education areas, 121-122

Ward, Douglas, 77
Windows, 10, 24, 28, 35, 41-43, 57, 66, 69, 73, 120
Wright, Henry, 77
Wulf, Kathleen M., 133
Wurtman, Richard, 95